THE LANDS OF THE LORDSHIP

THE ROMANCE OF ISLAY'S NAMES

by

DOMHNALL MACEACHARNA

Mellach lem bhith ind ucht ailiuin
    for beind cairrge,
Conacind and ar a mheinci
    féth na fairrci.

Conacind a tonda troma
    uas ler lethan,
Amail canait ceól dia n-athair
    for seól bethad.

                  (?) St. Columba.

---

[1] 'Tis pleasant in my opinion to be on an island's breast, on a peak of rock, that I might see, in all its changes, the aspect of the sea.

So that I might see its weighty waves o'er the broad main, how they sing music to their Father on life's voyage.

First Printed 1976

© Argyll Reproductions Ltd.

Published by

ARGYLL REPRODUCTIONS LTD.
Port Charlotte, Isle of Islay

Printed by Highland Printers Ltd., Diriebught Road, Inverness

INTRODUCTION

Man always seeks to impose his own personality upon his surroundings and, in the names he gives to the places he sees as he goes about his business, we can find clues to his outlook on life in general, to the extent of his powers of observation, to his religious values and to the general standards of his generation. The Latin playwright Terence, himself a freed slave wrote—and I paraphrase freely:—"Is that so far removed from your affairs that you don't need to bother about it? I am a human being and as far as I am concerned there is nothing relating to humanity that doesn't concern me." And this is true of place-names—these were given, not by shadowy ghosts or faceless map-makers, but by real, live, thinking human beings; people with all the good and bad in them that there is in ourselves. Further, Scottish place-names have an added interest for us in that the human beings who coined them were our own relations.

Again, when we think of "education", we normally think of it in terms of jotters, pencils and the three Rs, but there is another, a deeper education which our semi-literate society has all but lost.—An education so remote from us to-day that modern language does not even have a word to describe it. We can call it only "education from nature" or "learning from environment" or something equally flabby.

Even to-day there are many tribesmen in Africa and the South Sea Islands who, by our standards, are hopelessly ignorant—and, indeed, in many ways we are quite justified in describing them as ignorant; they lack our knowledge of mathematics, of formal grammar, even of our "humanity", yet these same men and women will survive where we would perish miserably from hunger and exposure. This is not just because they know how to light a fire without matches and which plants can safely be eaten, it is because they identify themselves with their environment in a way we can never hope to do. They can appreciate the "thinking" of the world around because they are "in" it—not "above" it, as sort of lords of creation. Not only so, but they have no need for tavern, television or even bingo: they can entertain themselves from a fund of unwritten, but well-loved literature passed down from father to son—or, more often, from grandmother to grandchildren, from the remotest past. And, when they do happen to go to a dance, they understand, not just how to go through the motions of the dance, but what the steps symbolise. That is the sort of education the givers of most of Islay's place-names had. That is why the older names seem to "merge into" their environment and, conversely, why modern names seem to jar upon us. That is why it is wiser, if you have a house needing a name, to consult the locals to find what that field or dell "used to be called" rather than try to invent your own. A casual glance at some of the utter horrors this island has to offer will convince you of the truth of that.

Far from being stupider than us, our forebears have much to tell us and tell us they will if we can approach them with humility, "think" ourselves into their shoes and see the world as they saw it.

In writing this book I have been helped by many people, far more than I can name. I must, however, mention Gilbert Clerk, Port Charlotte; Margaret Earl, Port Ellen and Alasdair MacEachern and Duncan MacGregor of Kilmeny who have made available to me their vast store of knowledge of this place and its past. I must thank Captain Donald, Port Charlotte, whose challenging views have often forced me to think again, and more deeply and, although I have often disagreed with him, I am conscious of a debt of gratitude to him. I must also thank Mr Joel MacManus for his very excellent illustrations and Mr Colin Roy for undertaking the work of publication. Finally, I must thank my wife for patiently reading the text of the work and for enduring with forebearance the long waits, the wasted meals and the general untidiness inseparable from the preparation of any book.

Keills, 1976.

Contents

CHAPTER 1

STRUCTURE OF AN ISLAND

Through uncountable ages the earth has spun round its parent sun. Countless millions of summer suns have warmed the rocks of this island—expanding them by day, cooling them by night until the contorted particles split asunder to give us the jagged rocks which defy the Atlantic breakers. Millions of winter showers have polished and rounded the hills which rise triumphantly towards Heaven. And all the time the hammer-blows of the surf have probed and prodded, ever searching for weaknesses to exploit, moving pebbles here, piling sand there. Already Islay is worn down to rocks so old that their history reaches past the scale of human imagining. It is only fairly recently in their lifetime that living creatures have appeared on earth and it is but as a few seconds ago that they have felt human footsteps. A few more million years and even these mighty rocks will have worn away and Islay will vanish beneath the waves which she has so long defied.

It really is hard to realise that humans arrived so recently in Islay that the island they saw is virtually unchanged from what we see. Man has built a few roads and houses, he has drained a few fields and plundered some rock, but that is about all. The whole of human history, perhaps the whole of Life itself is as if on a pitch black night a light flared up and was instantly extinguished. It is hard if to accept our utter insignificance in the scheme of things and to grasp the fact that, far from man moulding the land to suit his needs, the land has moulded him, deciding where he shall and shall not live, deciding the quality of the food on his table and the standard of the home he lives in

What changes have taken place in these last few thousand years? When man first came, Lochindaal ran slightly deeper inland between Blackrock and Springbank, the Laggan entered the sea rather further eastwards (it is still encroaching on the rich lands to the West) and Kilchoman Bay was a good deal more "bag" shaped, with the Crosprig rocks forming a promontory.

There was also a lot more woodland. The level ground from Ardilistry to Ardtalla was quite densely wooded: remains of this forest survive to the present day in Coille nam Bruthach—the Forest of the Braes. Several other areas sheltered from the west winds were also covered with scrub woodland.

To the early settlers woodland presented no problems. They got much of their food from hunting and the forest was the place where game abounded. Quite a different matter was the marshland. Islay is formed almost entirely of

7

hard, impermeable rock, and drainage, under natural conditions, is slow. To this day, in spite of ambitious reclamation programmes over the past twoh undred years, much of the surface of the island is quaking morass carrying a thick and still increasing cover of peat.

For our first human settlers then, the most valuable lands were the raised beaches, where sea-food was always to be had; the forest with its herds of game, and the sheltered grasslands of the lower slopes where they could graze their cattle and even try a little tentative cultivation, though this last was a rather ambitious matter, an unnecessary luxury. It will be remembered too, that the human has emerged as the dominant form of life during the closing period of one of the several ice-ages which have hit this world: 3,000-4,000 years ago the climate was colder than to-day. This hindered the development of agriculture in northern lands. Agriculturists appear first at a date earlier than 5ooo B.C. in northern Mesopotamia, Iran, Jordan and Turkey (See Glyn Daniel: First Civilisations in Pelican Series).

The next folk to come were rather wealthier, and wealth always brings its own problems for it is necessary for the "Haves" to protect themselves from the "Proposing to gets". For a pre-lock-and-key era this could be done either by settling on a small islet (or, if necessary, building one) or by enclosing the top of a steep-sided hillock which an enemy would find it hard to approach.

One more thing was essential for the protection of wealth and that was a large family. The more sons one had the safer one was and here we must mention the vast change which has taken place in family organisation over the past few hundred years. A glance at the Book of Genesis is enough to show that the type of family organisation known to Abraham, Isaac and Jacob was very different indeed from anything we know to-day though, since the writers do not make any comment on it, we may assume that it was a way of life well-known and accepted in their time. The family that they knew was patriarchal—ruled over by the eldest male of the group (rarely it was matriarchal)—all members of the family, irrespective of age or ability, were under the rule of the patriarch—even middle-aged married men, for reasons of family security, had to submit to the rule of the tyrant patriarch. New families were founded by younger sons who, seeing no prospect of becoming leader of the group themselves, set off on their own. Thus in the Genesis stories we are inclined to imagine Reuben as being, perhaps, in his teens and Joseph as seven or eight, but in fact, Reuben was approaching what, at that time was middle age and Joseph was seventeen when he was sold into slavery.

This ancient type of family organisation survived in Scotland in a modified form in the so-called "clan-system" down till the end of the 18th century.

The reasons for this patriarchal form of society were, as has been said, largely defensive; the family had to be protected at all costs and it was in the interest of all to keep it so. Grandfather and sons must buy as many wives as the family budget would allow, both to provide children and to form defensive bonds in the district. Anyone whose connection with a local group was unknown, would find himself, like Ishmael, with every man's hand against him. Notice that in ancient languages "enemy" and "stranger" are synonymous terms.

8

The food gatherer, the hunter and also the herdsman must be mobile. Not for them the well-built house and the comfortable chair—they must always be ready to move on, to look for game or to look for grass and, if a stronger family group appears, to be ready to move away swiftly. It is not till the food grower, the cultivator of the soil, appears that people can afford to settle down in one place and amass possessions which will make life pleasanter. It is to this transition period that these dozens of tiny forts or duns (doons) all over Islay belong. We will look more closely at them later but it is worth noting that they span a period of hundreds, perhaps thousands of years and we should not make the very common error of imagining that they were all occupied at the same time or by the same peoples. Unfortunately the very nature of their situation makes it rare for anything of any interest or value to be found in them and a vast field of study awaits the man prepared to seek evidence from which to date and classify them.

The Dark Ages were as dark in Islay as elsewhere, yet most of the modern development of the island was initiated during this twilight period. The parish boundaries were settled, the main farms were marked off and valued and the sites of the steadings settled. Further, the main lines of the road system were laid down. Only one great change has occurred since and that is the change in the cultivation pattern; large open fields on the level ground have replaced the old communal strips of cultivated land on the hill slopes. The field drain was an invention as revolutionary as the plough!

Finally we must realise that place names are most abundant where people live and where people live is determined by the soil. Soil is always deepest and richest on the lower ground where it has been washed from the surrounding hills. From the farmer's point of view there are three main types of soil:—

1—Sand

2—Loam

3—Clay

Sand, in this sense, is mainly large grains of silicon oxide derived from the breakdown of old igneous rock. It can be a heartbreak to the farmer as water percolates rapidly through it, carrying expensive fertilisers off to the sea and, of course, leaving plant-life to be parched during dry weather.

Clay consists of various forms of aluminium silicates also derived from old igneous rock but, unlike sand, with particles so small that they remain permanently in suspension in water (colloid solution). Clay soil, since there are so few air spaces, is heavy in weight and so, expensive to plough. It is hard to drain but once it has dried it will form a hard crust which tender shoots cannot penentrate.

Loam is what every farmer wants—but only wealthy ones can get—a perfect mixture of sand and clay having all the good points of both with none of the bad points of either. As one might expect, the best loamy soils in Islay lie in the Bridgend area, the area round Islay House, where hill clays, limestones and sand have mingled to produce the rich, green pastures of Eallabus.

9

However, even the best soils are of little value unless the underlying rock is suitable. Generally speaking, farmers want porous, sedimentary rock rather than the hard, impermeable, igneous rock. A rock, in other words, which will allow excess surface water to filter away and will not retain it until it becomes sour and acid. Acid soils are of little value for commercial cropping. If nature is unable to wash away the growth of previous years it will lie as a thick, sour mat of half-rotten material which we call peat. Much of Islay is covered with a superficial layer of peat, varying from a few inches to many feet in depth. We need not look for many human habitations among the peat hags! Only the poorest sort of farmers have ever lived there but, early last century, many poor folk were "settled" by the lairds on the peat between Duich and Glenegidale. The remains of their wretched habitations are worthy of examination being, as they are, a monument to human callousness.

CHAPTER 2

THE LANGUAGE

It is sometimes asserted by mis-guided patriots that the West Highlanders are a "pure" Celtic people whose "pure" language, Gaelic, has been spoken in Scotland from time immemorial: "writ in the rock" says one authority. This sort of stuff is never to be taken too seriously. The West Highlanders are a mixture of the small, dark pre-historic folk with conquering Celts of various sorts and Norsemen plus Lowland Scots and English settlers. Their language contains borrowings from Welsh, Norse and Latin and a huge mass of part-assimilated English words.

The Gaelic language, far from being "writ in the rock" was introduced from Northern Ireland about the 5th Century A.D. At that time groups of Gaelic-speaking settlers from a small, semi-independent Ulster kingdom called Dal Riata sailed across and established themselves in the district now known, correctly, as Argyll (Earra-Ghaidheal = the Bounds of the Gaels) and, absurdly, as West Strathclyde.

Dal Riata in Scotland soon gained its independence and eventually became the dominant state which unified our nation.

In order to understand the names of places, some knowledge of the language is necessary. Almost all Islay names are either Gaelic or have been moulded to fit the Gaelic phonetic system. Gaelic is a language of a very ancient type: it preserves features already obsolete in Latin and Greek of the time of Christ. In addition since it was the first Indo-European language to be spoken in Western Europe, it has picked up, from the older languages, features not found in other I.E. languages, though they are found in Eastern (Semitic) tongues.

For our purposes, it is unnecessary to cover much of the actual grammer but we must grasp the fact that place-names generally consist of two parts, viz. a generic element; hill; glen; farm; town, etc. and a descriptive element; black; cow; windmill; John's and so we get Blackhill, Cowglen, Windmill Farm, Johnston. The generic element must be a noun, the descriptive element may be either an adjective or a noun in the genitive (possessive) form.

In Gaelic the descriptive element normally follows, in Norse and English it precedes:—

Baile Mór (bally more)—Big town Lit. town big (Gaelic)

Ár Oss   (are awe-ss) — River Mouth (Norse)
                Bridgend (English)

To represent the sounds of Gaelic in a book is impossible because the range of sounds is much wider than in English, and only a native speaker can tell you the correct pronunciation, but here are some notes which will give general guidance:—

(1) There are 18 letters in the alphabet: j, k, q, v, w, x, y, z are absent.

(2) Each consonant has its radical form which has much the same sound as in English and also its aspirated or lenited form (adjectives are aspirated after a feminine noun):—

b-   bh-   v.
c-   ch-   ch as in loch.
d-   dh-   y before i and e (gh as in "ugh" before a, o, u).
f-   fh-   always silent in nouns.
g-   gh-   almost the same as dh-.
m-   mh-   v but with some air going through the nose.
p-   ph-   f as in pharmacy.
s-   sh-   h.
t-   th-   h.

Notice that sh- and th- do not have the same sounds as in English.

Let's try some actual names of places:—

Ile—(ee-le)—Islay; Muile—(moole)—Mull.

Alba—(alapa)—Scotland; Éire—(air-e)—Ireland.

Sasann—(sa-san)—England; A' Chuimre—(u chooymre)—Wales.

Port an Easa—(pawrt un ay-sa)—Waterfall Harbour.

Here are some useful place-name words:—

abhuinn (aving)—river.
àird (aarst)—a prominent height.
baile (bally)—a town.
bealach (be-alach)—pass, opening.
caisteal (kastyal)—castle.
cnoc (kr-awe-hk)—hill (watch the -n- which sounds -r-).
coille (coll-ye)—wood, forest (not timber).
creag (kray-hk)—rock.
doire (dor-e)—grove.
drùim (dream)—ridge of rock.
dùn (doon)—hill fort.
eilean (ail-ang)—island.
geodha (gee-oh-a)—creek, inlet.
gleann (glenn)—glen, valley.
loch (loch)—loch, lake.
machair (ma-chair)—coastal plain.
maol (moo-al)—rounded hill, rounded promontory.
monadh (mon-ugh)—moorland.
port (paw-rt)—port, harbour, bay.
rudha (roo-ah)—headland, promontory.
sgeir (scare)—reef.
sliabh (slee-uv)—hill slope.
tigh (tie)—house.

tobar (toe-par)—well.
tràigh (try)—beach.
And some adjectives:—
àluinn (aal-uing)—beautiful.
àrd (aart)—high.
beag (bake)—small.
caol (keul as in Fr. feu)—narrow.
cas (kass)—steep.
fada (fata)—long.
mór (more)—big.
Colours:—
bàn (baan)—fair, white.
buidhe (boo-y)—yellow.
donn (down)—brown.
dubh (doo)—black.
gorm (gorum)—blue (of sea) green (of grass).
liath (lee-ah)—grey.
ruadh (roo-ah)—red.
Finally:—
(1) "the" is rather difficult in Gaelic. Usually it is "an" or " a' " (un, u).
(2) -ll- is sounded as in "million".
And to try out our new-found knowledge on some real Islay names:—
Port Bàn (pawrt baan)—the White Port.
An Àird Bheag (un aarst vake)—the Little Headland.
Am Bealach Ruadh (um be-alach roo-ah)—the Red Pass.
An Druim Dubh (un dream doo)—the Black Ridge.
Gleann Mhàrtuin[1] (glenn vaart-inn)—Martin's Glen.

Like rocks, place-names occur in strata. As one group of people after another takes possession of the land each leaves its own impression in the form of names. Of course, a new population with a new language will give its own, new names: the old inhabitants of the area have been slain or enslaved and masters do not learn the slaves' language, but names of major features especially tend to "stick". The new masters ask the older folk: "What do you call that hill, farm, etc.?" and the name, suitably moulded to fit the phonetics of the new language, lives on. In this way a language may be completely lost, its very name forgotten, yet the names its speakers gave to the natural features they saw around them live obstinately on. Even in such a small area as Scotland we can discern layer upon layer of place-names and, just as the types of rock vary from district to district, so too do the place-names. To take a simple example, the word "aber" was used in both the Pictish and Welsh languages (which closely resembled each other) for a river mouth. This word occurs fairly frequently throughout the Pictish areas but it is rare or unknown in other areas of the British Isles except in Wales itself and in the West Highlands there is one solitary example, Applecross.

In general, however, Scotland shows six clear layers of names:—
(1) Prehistoric names: (Ben) Ledi, Hebrides, Inellan (some experts say that this last is Gaelic, Island, but where is the island?) and, perhaps, Lewis.

Apart from the relatively small number of prehistoric names all other names in Scotland are Indo-European in origin (except a few given last century by returned pensioned-off empire-builders and the like such as Abyssinia) so we must say a word or two about the Indo-European peoples. . . .

At a vague date in the remote past some long-forgotten upheaval in the East uprooted a very rough and vicious tribe (the members of which may have called themselves the Aryans or something of the sort). This tribe proceeded to attack its more peaceful neighbours, overcoming and enslaving them and then moving on to seek fresh adventures. The tribe soon broke into separate groups, one of which moved south and entered India (these are now the Hindus and their cousins) but the main movement was westward (Why is it that the centres of civilisation tend to move westward, the better areas of almost any town are the western parts and emigrating folk prefer to move to a western land?).

By the time that Moses was leading the Children of Israel out of Egypt these Aryans had grabbed much of Asia Minor and Syria—(these were the O.T. Hittites and they were in Anatolia not later than about 1900 B.C. being centred in the bend of the Halys River). Not long after they entered Greece where we know them as the Mycenaeans of the Trojan Wars and it is worth noticing that the pre-Indo-Europeans survived in Greece right down to the Classical Period. (Heroditus calls them the Pelasgians. From them we get such words as hyacinth and labyrinth). Next they entered Western Europe, overrunning what are now Italy, France, Spain: another group seized Germany and Holland and yet others moved north and west into Russia, Poland and Czechoslovakia. Finally, the roughest, toughest most aggressive elements among them made their way to the very edge of the world; to Scandinavia and the British Isles. These last are our ancestors. We to-day call them all the Indo-European peoples.

Indo-European (Aryan)

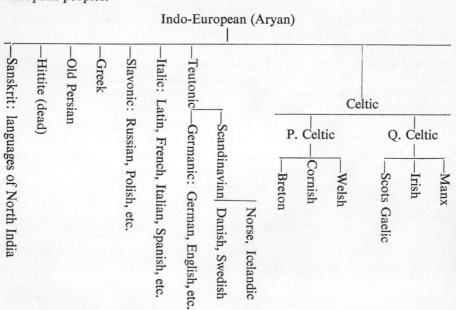

14

Here is the Indo-European "family tree". The Celts (Caesar's Gauls) settled in the areas now known as France, Belgium, Switzerland, Northern Italy (Vergil's tutor was Gaulish), the Iberian Peninsula and, of course, Britain and Ireland, with smaller colonies elsewhere—including the district round Ankara where they were visited by St. Paul who, it will be recalled, describes them as "foolish Galatians"![2]

Q Celtic preserves the ancient I.E. q sound which becomes p or b in the P group, e.g. Gaelic mac (son), anciently maqos, appears in Modern Welsh as mab. No ancient Gaelic word contains p e.g. athair, iasg = Latin: pater, piscis = English father, fish. Words containing p are borrowings; e.g. pòg = kiss, from Latin, pax = peace.

Almost all the languages of Modern Europe are of the Indo-European family and, indeed, it is most interesting to trace words from language to language. For example, if we take the Latin word "rex", a king, this is obviously the same word as the French "roi" and the Gaelic "rìgh" and, slightly less obviously, the same word as the German "Reich" and the English "rich". If we think of the English word "water" this is obviously the same as the German "Wasser" and if we remember the Hittites from our Old Testament readings, their word was "Vadâr". As one German writer puts it: "how staggering to realise that, with three thousand years intervening, a Frisian living on the North Sea coast of Germany, and a Pennsylvania Dutchman of Eastern North America (and, he might have added, an Ileach from Bowmore) would understand a Hittite's cry of thirst!".[3]

Languages which do *not* belong to this family are Finnish and Hungarian which, with one or two others, are spoken by the descendents of the Huns and other tribes from the Far East. The most interesting non-Indo-European language by far found in Europe is the Basque language, which appears to be a genuine descendent of the ancient tongues spoken before the conquering Aryans arrived.

We can now move on to the other layers of names:—

(2) Proto-Celtic. Very early Indo-European type names. These names were given by a people who were nature worshippers and, in consequence, most surviving names of this group are river, i.e. life-goddess names:—

Dee, Don—both from Devona (as in Devon)—Goddess.
Cart   —the Cleansing Goddess (cf. cartin' the byre).
Boyne   —the Cow Goddess.
Ness   —a feminine word of unknown meaning—it may be the descriptive element in Islay's Ardnis).

In this connection no one has ever explained why there is a Black Cart and a White Cart, a Blackaddar and a Whitadder, a Findhorn (fionn-White) and a Deveron (dubh—black). It is probably a relic of a dualistic religion—the white, or fair one being the lucky one and the other the one of ill-omen.

(3) Cruithnean and Cymric. The two being almost impossible to separate. Both these groups are P Celtic (subject possibly to some qualification in the case of the former) and both entered Britain and spread to Ireland.

15

The earlier arrivals were the Cruithni, who appear to have taken over most of Britain from the dark-haired, non-I.E. peoples and the small I.E. "advance guard". These people appear to have called themselves PRITANI, or something of the sort, and from this, of course, comes the name BRITAIN. At a later date the Q Celts made this into Qritani—Cruitani—Cruithni, and so Cruithentuath, the Gaelic for Pictland. It will be remembered that the Pictish king whom Columba met was called Brude—there were several of the name—and this appears to be a form of the old group name, containing, as it does, the consonants of Br-t(d). The Irish is Bruide, which points the same way. Another common name among these Cruithni was Drest (the vowel varies, becoming Drost in Irish) with its diminutive or by-form Drostan. This name occurs several times as the name of Pictish kings; it occurs in the very first piece of extant Gaelic written within Scotland—a short history of the Cistercian abbey at Deer, written during the reign of David I—1124–1153, where the original abbey is said to have been founded by Columba and a certain Drostan Mac Cosgreg. Interestingly, the same name appears in Cornwall where, near the "Arthurian" site known as Castle Dore stands a monolith bearing the inscription DRUSTANUS HIC IACIT FILIUS CUNOMORI (here lies Drustan, son of Cynvawr). This is believed to be the original of Tristram, the follower of Arthur. Cynvawr, presumably the other man named here, reigned in Dumnonia (S.W. England) about 540 A.D.

The Cruithni held certain animals sacred and it would appear that each tribe had its own totem animal. Thus, in Scotland, we find that the Gaelic name for the former Pictish region known now as Sutherland is Cataibh. This is a Locative Plural = Among the Cat (folk). The lands of this tribe appear to have stretched to John o' Groats because when, at a later date, the Norse seized that North-East corner of the Mainland, they named it Katta (gen. pl.) Nes = Cats' Point = Caithness, while the lands lying to the south of the ness they named Sudrland = Southland = Sutherland. The Gaels meantime re-named the north-east corner Gallaibh = Among the Foreigners.

We find also Arcaibh = Orkney = Among the Pig (folk) while there is mention also of Sheep folk and, in Ireland, Salmon folk, but the one which is of real interest to us occurs in Ptolemy: EPIDION AKRON = Horse Promontory = Kintyre. That Ptolemy was correct can be proved by the corresponding Irish name Aird Echde = Kintyre, with the same meaning. This name points to the existence of a Horse folk as the ruling tribe in the peninsula and we may assume the Kintyre family MacEachern, Mackechnie, (Horse Lord's son) to be descended from this Cruithnean tribe. Ptolemy lived about 130 A.D.

Distinctive Cruithnean type names are common only in the North-East where the best-known is "pit" = a portion of land (cognate with "piece"): Pitfuar, Pittenwemyss, and so on (this element is not found in Argyll); and names such as Lovat which can be matched by Islay's Lossit (lossaid) probably from a stem in -ant-.

The Cymri, Gaelic Cuimrich, who are the same folk as the Belgae whom Caesar disliked so much, and the Fir Bolg of ancient Irish stories, entered South

16

Britain, displacing their Cruithnean cousins northwards. They settled at least as far north as Glen Falloch where we have Clach nan Breatann—Britons' Stone, and the south bank of Forth. In Ireland they seized Leinster and some other areas.

When, in 43 A.D., Claudius sent his legions to occupy Britain, it was these Cymri whom they met. The Roman advance in South Britain has been carefully studied. It was a slow and bitterly-fought campaign—grim traces of that advance have been found at Maiden Castle, Dorset and other sites—but by about 80 A.D. Agricola's forces were in touch with the Cruithni. In spite of their staggering losses of territory they were very far from being cowed or subdued and, after several determined efforts on the part of the Romans, the attempt to reduce North Britain was abandoned as was the projected occupation of Ireland. Apart from a few punitive raids, no Roman soldier entered the northern parts of Britain and, as far as we know, there were no military operations in the Western Isles at all, though there is some evidence for trips of exploration.

When finally, after more than three hundred years, the Romans started to withdraw, the people of South Britain found themselves in a very difficult situation. For years past the coastal areas had been subjected to irritating raids by Irish and Continental pirates and the northern defensive wall had been overrun on several occasions. Now, while the British princes squabbled among themselves, the heathen roamed at will over the land.

In 383 the Army in Britain proclaimed its own emperor, a man of obscure origins called Maximus and he led off the best of the troops to enforce his claim. As could have been expected, he and his troops were scattered and killed and a sadly weakened Britain appealed frantically for help. About 399 a small policing operation was carried out by Rome which dealt effectively with the Irish but the overwhelming Teutonic invasion of Gaul about this time left Britain worse off than before. The Teutonic savages could not be tamed as easily as the rather more civilised Irish.

Faced with this thorny problem the remnants of the Army in Britain did not hesitate: they proclaimed another emperor—Constantine III—and went off to fight for him. They were, of course, defeated and dispersed and Britain lay defenceless.

A big Saxon raid about 410 brought home to people the grave danger of their situation and, with a rare show of unity, they declared the Independence of Britain and undertook a national scheme of defence. The distracted Emperor Honorius could only express his delight at being relieved of *one* worry.

At this time there appeared an interesting, though enigmatic character calling himself Pelagius. He caused much worry in the official Church by his unorthodox version of Christianity. Pelagius denied the Doctrine of Original Sin, pointing out that a God who is Perfection could create only that which is perfect. St. Augustine and Pelagius clashed violently on the subject while the gentle St. Jerome went so far as to describe poor Pelagius as "a most obstinate, porridge-fed Scot". The Pelagian Heresy "caught on" in Britain, however, and a Rome which could not spare a single soldier for Imperial defence hastened to send missionaries to protect the Britons from doctrinal error. This well-meant zeal served only to create new divisions at the very time when national survival, and even life itself, depended on unity.

From now on the story of the P Celts is one of unrelieved gloom. The Cruithni were reduced to the area now remembered as Pictland with "islands" in Galloway and one or two other places.

The Picts defended themselves bravely. Valuable breathing-time was gained when the Northumbrian Ecgfrith marched his armies to disaster outside Forfar (685 A.D.). For a time the credit of the Pictish monarchy rose. There seems to have been a defeat of invaders from Dal Riada about the same time. Half a century later the Picts took the offensive. Angus I invaded Dal Riada and took Dùn Add, the capital, in 736. A year or two later he was active in the West again. The Annals of Ulster have "Percussio Dalriatai" under 741. Eventually, of course, the Picts had to succumb to the rather superior religion and culture of Dal Riada. Political unity was effected under Kenneth I during the 840s and after that mentions of Picts become uncommon and eventually cease altogether.

As for the Cruithni of Galloway, they seem simply to have withered away. By the 18th century they were reduced to the status of a tinker tribe (Trotter's Galloway Gossip) and, until recent years "Pecht" remained as a term of contempt and abuse in Southern Scotland.

In the South, Continental raiders seized Kent about 450 and, after a battle at Crayford in 457, the Cymri fled to London. For the next few years South Britain knew only rape and pillage, but by the 460s, defence of a sort had been organised under a certain Ambrosius and a measure of prosperity began to creep back. The end of the century saw a return to bad times with the heathen seizing land on all sides but, after a battle at a place called Mons Badonicus— probably to the west of Reading, the advance halted for about forty years (circa 514–547). The advance then resumed and the collapse of the entire South-West came in 658 when Cenwalh stormed into central Somerset.

Further north things had already reached disaster proportions. A determined effort to get a united front to drive out the invaders, who had already seized most of the East Coast from the Humber to the Forth, ended in utter and complete defeat at Catterick about 600. The tiny kingdom of Elmet nestling amoung the Pennines was now left defenceless and succumbed about sixteen years later. The main defences were down and all South Britain, save only the extreme West was lost for ever. Angle Northumbria was now ready to deal with Strathclyde, the last remaining stronghold in that part of Britain and Fate loaded the dice still more heavily against the unfortunate Cymri of Strathclyde. Dal Riada formed bonds of friendship with Northumbria, partly through a mutual interest in Christian education! These Scots of Dal Riada had long cast covetous eyes on the fertile lands bordering the Firth of Clyde which lay so near and yet so far. Now seemed the ideal opportunity. A series of vicious attacks was launched on the unfortunate Cymri but, by one of these miracles which sometimes happen, the Cymri, with the courage of despair, hit back and slew Domhnall Breac, King of Dal Riada in the valley of Carron in 642. He was a famous man, grandson of St. Columba's friend Aidan and his death appears to have demoralised Dal Riada for many years to come. Miraculously too, although the Angles infiltrated the north shore of Solway and into Galloway (the Angle, St. Cuthbert (635–687) is commemorated in Kirkcudbright = St. Cuthbert's Church), they seem to have been held out of the lands of Kyle and Carrick. Cunningham too, in spite of its name, shows few signs of Angle occupation. The region of Strathclyde continued independent until 1018 when it was incorporated into Scotland as a semi-independent principality. The last mention of it as a national entity known to me is in a charter of David I for the founding of Glasgow Cathedral where he signs himself Prince of Cumbria.

To-day only Wales and Britanny remain as centres of P Celtic speech and, regrettably, French Government policy apparently aims at the extirpation of the Breton speakers. England, as ever, takes no active steps but waits patiently for the death of the Welsh language.

Cymrian type names are fairly plentiful in former Strathclyde. Aber (G. inver = river mouth) is rare outside the Pictish areas but we find caer = fort as in Carlisle, Carlaverock, etc.; eglyws = church as in Ecclefechan = Little Church; tref = township Ochiltree = High Village; pen = head as in Penpont = Bridgend.

Pelagius is a puzzle. His name means "Born of the Sea" — a good old pagan name—and is exactly the same as the Welsh name Morgan. On the other hand, the Mackays, who belong to the extreme north-west of Scotland are frequently called Clanna Mhorgain. We could agree that he must be a native of Britain and indeed he is described as a "British monk". Unfortunately, Jerome calls him a Scot and at that period "Scot" should = "Irish". It certainly did not have its modern meaning in the 5th century.

(4) Gaelic. The Gaels, like their predecessors, the P Celts came from some unknown point on the Continent, possibly the Iberian Peninsula, but they by-passed Britain and landed in Ireland—probably on the East Coast. They seem to have seized the district of the Pale and to have fanned out into the Midlands. The last part of Ireland to fall was, traditionally, Ulster. Its capital, Emain Macha is said to have fallen to Colla Uais, claimed as an ancestor of Clan Donald, round about 329 A.D.

By the time of Christ, Ireland, like Britain, had at least four distinct groups of inhabitants viz. The non-Indo-European aboriginal inhabitants, the Cruithni (whom we think of as the Picts in Scotland), the Cymrian P Celts and now, recently arrived, the Gaels. The coming of the Gaels forced many of the people of the older groups to flee or to abandon their traditional way of life if they stayed. Gaelic's "kitchen" vocabulary contains several P Celtic borrowings, pointing to the enslavement of the captured womenfolk.

Among those who fled before the Gaels was a group of non-Indo-Europeans whom we know as the Fir Iboth. A corruption of their name gives us the word Hebrides—and incidentally, tells us where they fled to. The large number of obscure names in the Cowal peninsula too may well be a record of part of this, or some similar group of fugitives, speaking a long-forgotten tongue.

By the third or fourth century after Christ these Irish Gaels and their erstwhile enemies, now largely assimilated, had raided and over-run a great deal of the western seaboard of Britain but their greatest, indeed their only lasting

19

success, was the establishment of an extension of the Ulster kingdom of Dal Riada to the West Highlands. The Dal Riada were probably Erenn, a P Celtic people now speaking the language of the conquerors. It is sad to have to point out that the Scottish Gael, the hero of many a bloody field, the builder of England's empire, the man of whom General Wolfe said "an excellent fighter and no great hurt if he falls", was perhaps not really a Gael at all!

Irish tradition tells how Cairbre Riata moved, with his people, from Munster to the extreme north of Ulster and even across into Kintyre and the West of Scotland. His descendents, the sons of Erc, continued the work and eventually Columba negotiated political autonomy for Scottish Dal Riada. In point of fact, Cairbre is a very obscure person indeed. He is really no more than the eponymous ancestor of the tribe; a figure of myth and legend rather than flesh and blood. All this story tells us is about the pre-Gaelic natives, driven to the extreme bounds of their own land and even beyond these bounds by the pressure of political events, finally losing even their own identity and becoming fused with the conquerors.

There are plenty of Irish tales recording raids on Kintyre and the Isle of Man including one of the taking of a fort—probably Dunaverty is the fort in question —and the carrying off of the chief's daughter, Blàthnaid—Little Flower. While we need not doubt that these raids were taking place probably from a very early date, the main invasion of Argyll took place late in the fifth century—or early in the sixth.[4] The prime movers are supposed to have been Fergus, Loarn and Angus said, though there seems some doubt on the subject, to have been the sons of Erc. Notice here the most unusual name Loarn (from which we get the modern Lorne). It does not seem to be Gaelic at all. While the dates and, indeed, the facts are rather confused in the records, it would appear that Domingort, son of Fergus, reigned as a true king in what is now Argyll.[5]

According to mid-Argyll tradition, which it seems pointless to question, the invaders landed at Crinan, over-ran the Moine Mhór and seized the hill-fort of Dùn Add, which they made their capital. Since these are the very founders of Scotland and since Dùn Add is therefore Scotland's first capital, surely these are names every Scot ought to reverence. How many have even heard of them?

It is said that Dùn Add means the Long Fort and that it takes its name from the River Add. This is, to say the least of it, open to question as, in the Gaelic of these times, the Long Fort would have been Dún Fóta, and in our oldest mention of it (when it was besieged in 683) this is recorded as "Obsesio Duin ATT". Further, the modern form ought to be Dùn Fad. It is indeed most likely that dùn and river names are the same: it would be a most amazing co-incidence if they were not, but that name is not "fada"—long. Probably it is another pre-Gaelic, and possibly pre-Indo-European name.

Be that as it may, the three made this place their base for future operations and within a short space of time they and their immediate descendents had occupied the whole area of modern Argyll except, perhaps, for some of the islands.

In the share-out, Fergus, the eldest got Knapdale and Kintyre with Cowal, most of the rest went to Loarn, and Islay went to Angus, but apparantly

20

he was unable to occupy it except for a tiny corner. Two generations later, the grandsons of Fergus, Gabhran and Comgall divided the area claimed by their grandfather. Gabhran took Mid Argyll, Knapdale and Kintyre while Comgall took the peninsula which still bears his name, Cowal. It is not known definitely who took the other isles.

The position in Islay is more than obscure. It is said that it was the great-great grandsons of Angus who finally took possession of the island and in the account given in Accalamh fir nAlban the lands of Cinel Aonghuis are mentioned separately. As far as one can judge, it would seem that the original settlers did no more than hold their own while a group of their descendants cleared the remainder and settled the conquered land. One account actually maintains that they did not conquer it but inherited it from a Cruithnean (Pictish) ancestress.

As will have been realised by now, the dating of the invasion is in doubt but it can hardly have been earlier than, say, 450 A.D. nor later than 500 A.D. It took place after Christianity had been brought to Ireland and by the time Columba came, circa 563, the Isles were settled and peaceful under the "new management". Columba was able to move about without let or hindrance and live in a totally undefended island but his biographer does remark casually on the fact that he did need an interpreter now and then when talking to the local folk (Cf. story of Artbranan: in Adomnan).

(5) Norse and Danish. Again the two groups are so closely related that it is often difficult or impossible to separate them. The Scots and Irish distinguished two types: Fionn Ghoill—Fair foreigners, who are generally assumed to be the Norse, and Dubh Ghoill—Dark foreigners, probably the Danes. This latter lives on in the surname MacDougall, though they were not Danes but of mixed Norse–Gaelic ancestry, being descended from Dougall, the eldest son of that Somerled, King of the Isles, who was killed near the site of the present Glasgow Airport in 1164.

In general it is in the North, and West that we find Norse names and in the South of Scotland, and North of England that we find Danish. As far as Islay is concerned, we can regard all the names of this stratum as being Norse and all belonging to the period circa 850–1100. After the opening of the 12th century Gaelic seems to have re-asserted itself as the Norse influence from the homeland weakened and the Isles moved closer to complete autonomy. Norse influence finally ended and, indeed, the civil administration broke down completely after 1266 when, by the Treaty of Perth, the Isles were returned to a Scotland which had made no provision for governing them. The period of anarchy which followed boded ill for the future and, in fact, the turbulent conditions in the Isles were to give future Scottish kings much food for thought![6]

(6) After the fall of the Norse kingdom in the West, a fresh layer of Gaelic names was laid down. It is to this layer that the vast majority of our field, hill and moorland names belong, but it is often hard to distinguish the new from the older and to say whether or not a name was given before the Norse period or after. As we shall see, it is usually possible to do so with church names as the introduction of Continental-style Roman Catholicism in the 12th century had

the effect of rendering obsolete part at least of the "vocabulary" of the older, monastic orientated church and so such a name as Beinn Bhiocaire (Ben Vicar, the Vicar's mountain) may reasonably be assumed to be a name given to replace a Norse name which, in turn, had displaced a still earlier name. In the same way, a very few names can be dated with reasonable certainty, Kyleakin, for example, Hakon's channel can be dated without much doubt to 1263, the year that Hakon passed Skye on his punitive expedition against Scotland which ended in disaster on the foreshore at Largs.

(7) The final layer of names in Scotland is the layer of English names. English was undoubtedly spoken within Scotland at a very early date giving us such names as Kelso, Jedburgh and the like. Probably by the latter part of the 11th century it had started to spread into the Central Lowlands, where we find such names as (Anglo-Saxon) Falkirk. The monasteries of the Middle Age helped to carry English northwards as did the Scottish kings' "divide and rule" policy of bringing in Norman landlords to break the power of the old, semi-independent Celtic mormaers.

At the time of the debacle of 1707, English had still not penetrated the West or North-West except for tiny pockets here and there and indeed it is probable that Gaelic was still quite widely spoken within walking distance of Glasgow Cross[7] as recently as 1745–6 when the whole position was changed. Probably Prince Charlie was not an agent provocateur, but the effect was the same. The London Government seized the opportunity to extirpate as many as possible of those who might in any way have been concerned in the "recent unnatural rebellion". The Highlanders were driven from their homes like cattle and new English-speaking settlers were "planted" throughout most of the Highland area. Islay was lucky. Far-sighted Campbell lairds would have nothing to do with Charlie's ridiculous rebellion and the English government had no reasonable excuse for plundering and devastating the island. Again, Islay was able, also largely through the good offices of the Shawfield Campbells, to escape the worst effects of the so-called Clearances and, although circumstances have brought Islay Gaelic to the verge of extinction to-day, the layer of English names is still very thin on the ground. Apart from one or two farm names such as "Woodend" we have little more than a few street names redolent of English suburbia (Hawthorn Terrace, Birch Drive, etc.) bestowed by altruistic gentlemen who shudder when they hear the barbarous noise of Western Europe's most ancient Indo-European language.

(a) To avoid confusion I have tried to avoid the vague term "British" to describe any early group of settlers. I have called the two main streams of P Celts Cruithni (with Pict for those settled in Scotland) and Cymri to describe the historic South Britons.

(b) In spite of dating difficulties, the Brude whom Columba knew as King of the Picts was probably a son of the famous Mailcon, King of Gwynedd (North Wales). He appears to have pushed the Dal Riadic settlers out of a fair part of their stolen lands. (Annals of Tigernach c. 559–60: Teichedh do Alban-chaib riam Bruidhi mac Maelchon righ Chruithnech).

There is no proof that Mailcon was the father of that Brude who met

22

Columba, in fact their datings do not agree very well for such a conjecture but: (1) Brude's father was *a* Mailcon and it was never a very common name and (2) Succession among the Picts was reckoned through the mother's and not the father's family. This being so, it was possible and even common for a Pictish king to be son of the King of another country.

If the conjecture is correct, Brude was no shaggy savage sunk in squalid heathenism, but rather the son of a cultured, well-educated Christian, a man trained by no less a person than the great St. Iltud of Llantwit Major, a man who had known King Arthur. Brude's conversion by Columba may have been little more than a pointing out of his duty to bring the Gospel to his own people.

[1] Here is a different, a rarer, cause of aspiration. Masculine proper nouns aspirate in the genitive singular.
[2] Galatians 3,1.
[3] Genesis 23, 3–18; Numbers: 13, 29; II Kings: 7,6.
[2] C. W. Ceram: Narrow Pass, Black Mountain.
[4] O'Rahilly—History and Mythology of Ancient Ireland.
[5] Chadwick—Early Scotland.
[6] In 1966 I pointed out that Argyllshire schools should celebrate by a holiday the 700th anniversary of our gaining Scottish nationality. It turned out, however, that although the councillors had heard of the English Magna Carta, and agreed that a school holiday would be appropriate to mark it, they had never heard of the Treaty of Perth. Quis custodiet ipsos custodes!
[7] North of the Clyde the names are largely of Gaelic origin: Duntocher, Gartnavel, Milngavie, Balmore, Kilbowie, Ardmore. Southwards the pattern changes with fewer modern-type Gaelic names and more Welsh or Welsh/English names: Linwood, Eaglesham, Cardonald.

CHAPTER 3

THE EARLIEST NAMES

In schooldays we learned of the three great pre-historic "Ages":—

Stone Age
Bronze Age
Iron Age

These names describe the types of materials used for tools and weapons at specific stages of a people's development: they are no indications of "when" things happened. Thus, in Palestine, the Hebrews took some nasty beatings from the Philistines and Canaanites whose development was slightly more advanced into the Iron Age; Scotland at that time was in the late Stone Age. To-day, we still can point to Australian aborigines who live in the Stone Age.

These names for the "Ages" are rather unfortunate because they tend to disguise much more significant aspects in human development than mere tools can show: vast and far-reaching changes in social organisation and metaphysical thought characterise these mis-named "Ages" and rather than think in terms of static "Ages" we should see streams of cultural development.

In the earliest of these Ages religion was purely utilitarian: moral and philosophical thought, insofar as they were known to all, being separate disciplines. The religion of the Stone Age was sympathetic magic aimed at increasing the food-supply. If, for example, one drew a picture of a deer on the ground of a "lucky" place and mimicked the actions of a successful hunt in a "dance" round the image, stabbing at it and concluding by capering round in a victory roll, bringing home the carcass, one could expect success in the actual hunt—strange to reflect that from these humble origins sprang the art of Pavlova and Nijinski! (Similarly, to make oneself brave, one could eat the flesh of a "brave" animal and, to gain wisdom and skill, one could absorb the flesh of a respected person—here too, in the squalor of the cannibal feast are the roots from which eventually grew the beauty of the Eucharist). It has been noted, in Australia and elsewhere, where the Stone Age customs still live, that certain little hollows in the rock are carefully reserved for the mixing of the very special paints needed for the drawings. It is not too difficult to imagine the savages of the Rhinns setting aside for their ceremonies the rock outside Kilchiaran Kirk with its little "cup marks". One thing certain is that at least some of the Christian sites of Islay were originally pagan places of worship.

The great scientific discovery of the Neolithic and early Bronze Age was not the principle of smelting metal but the significance of the sex act: in earlier Stone Age times its connection with reproduction was not even suspected. Having gained this new knowledge man, as is his wont, cast around in his mind for some way to turn the information to his advantage. Very soon various developments took place. No longer need man be dependent on the hunt. Now he could keep his own live-stock, breeding as required and, indeed, improving on nature's handiwork. Further, observing the significant fact of birth and growth in springtime man decided that this was due to the masculine and vigorous Sun overshadowing the female Earth, fertilising it through the streams and rivers. Thus was born the Earth Mother cult, perhaps the most important of all religions for the impact it made on human thought and Christianity itself owes a great debt to this first of the "world religions".

Let's consider the facts. In spring the days could be seen to be lengthening. The sun could be seen to be rising ever higher in the sky until, finally, at Midsummer Day it reached its zenith. Thereafter, it slowly receded, describing daily a shorter arc in the heavens until, by Midwinter, it seemed to "die", not moving either up or down for a couple of days. Then, mirabile dictu, the sun was reborn and began to reascend the heavens—hence the Papal choice of 25th December as Christmas, to mask the pagan Festival of the Unconquerable Sun.

The whole cycle, it was noted, took roughly 360 days to complete and could be divided into four sections of some 90 days of sub-circles each with its own characteristics and each of which came to develop its own festivals. In diagram form:—

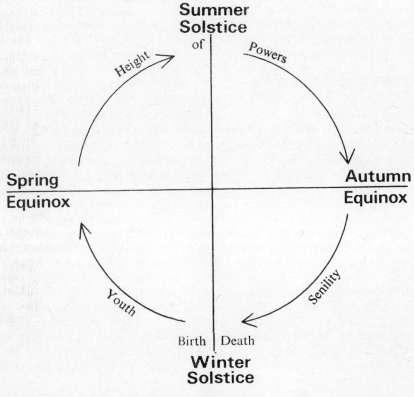

In this natural rhythm lie embedded many of the sub-strata of our civilisation. The Baal (or more correctly, Bel) religion of the Philistines, Tammuz of the Babylonians, the Kore and Demeter of Greece and many other gods and faiths sprang from it or rather, were woven around it. Bel was the young and handsome sky and weather god from whose lattice-windowed palace fell the life-giving rains. Eventually, however, Bel was attacked by his enemy, the dragon Mot who seized the terrified Bel and slew him. El, the ancient father of the gods, tore his clothes, gashed himself and mourned many days but, all was well. Bel was restored to life by the love of his sister who re-assembled his dismembered body and restored him to life, no longer weak and pusillanimous but again young, strong and vigorous. The tale of the contest on Mount Carmel illustrates this (I Kings XVIII), the priests gashing themselves and mourning then leaping up on to the altar to symbolise the re-birth.

The ancient name of Land's End was Belerion—(Place of Bel(er), while in Islay, an old tale tells how Godred Crovan (a Norseman!) slew a dragon which had its lair at Iomaire Chòmhnard—the Level Rig and those with imagination can still see the coils made by the dragon's body on the ground. Godred was, of course, a late substitution for the long-forgotten Bel.

According to the Greek story, Demeter and her daughter Kore were out in the fields when Kore suddenly vanished. It was later found that she had been stolen by the King of the Underworld. An arrangement was arrived at whereby the girl spent half the year with her mother and the other half in the Underworld, leaving her mother to mourn. When we realise that Demeter means Earth Mother, the meaning of the story becomes obvious. A form of this story hung on in the isles at least until the 18th century in the form of tales of the "Saint" Bride or, more properly the goddess Brigantia (the goddess of the tribe of the Brigantes).

Enough has been said to make it obvious that the devotees of this type of religion would need meeting places with solar and phallic symbols. The best European examples of solar symbols are to be seen in great circles at Stonehenge and Callarnish but Islay has a small circle at Cultuinn in the Rhinns. This"circle" actually an ellipse roughly 33×42 m with its main axis apparantly aligned on Slieve Snacht, Co. Donegal. The construction is dated with reasonable certainty to early in the second millennium B.C. A recent excavation by Dr Euan Mackie has shown that the site had assumed more or less its present ruinous form even before the peat began to grow. Some fallen stones rest directly on the old ground surface with no trace of peat under them. That means that the site had been abandoned even before King Solomon built his Temple in Jerusalem! A short causeway connects the high ground on which the circle stands to another "island" in the peat-bog which appears to have been a sanctuary. Vague and indeterminate traces of further structures are to be seen on the other side of the modern road.   Surprisingly, no specific name seems to be remembered for this circle. The name of the nearby farm, Cultuinn, might, it has been suggested, signify "Behind the Fires"=referring to the fires lighted at the circle which does, in fact, lie to the South. While there is no particular philological objection to this derivation, it must be admitted that it might equally well be a Norse name

"Hill"+Personal name: in this area Norse names do predominate. "Kelsa" is a Norse name which we shall look at later. It means Keel Farm because the Norse thought the standing stones looked like ships' keels—Cf. Callernish in Lewis.

On the left hand side of the Lagavullin Road, just outside Port Ellen, lies a most interesting field called Pàirc Bhaile Néill—The Field of Niall's Township, a relatively modern name. This field was in use as a sacred place at the time of the change-over to Christianity and has traces of both pagan and early Christian symbolism. The first, and most prominent object to be seen in the field is an immense and beautifully tapered standing-stone. Lying behind it is a little hillock some five or six feet high. This is known as Cnoc Mór—the Great Hill. These two represent the penis and the testicles. Some metres away, due north, lies a tiny, ancient chapel within a roughly circular sanctuary. Two curiously pierced stones guard the entrance to the sanctuary and looking due south between these stones at midday, one finds the standing stone and the sun forming a straight line. This chapel represents the female element. To the West, forming an almost exact equilateral triangle (again a female symbol) with the stone and the little chapel lies an ancient well of pure water. The name of the Chapel is Cille Lasrach =Lasair's Church and the well is called Tobar Cille Lasrach=the Well of Cille Lasrach (We will be saying something about this word "cille" in a moment). Lasrach is the genetive form of a feminine word meaning a flame. Here the marriage of ancient and uncouth paganism and modern European thought takes place=old and new are quite inextricably entangled and the folk tales told of this field reflect a vague memory of human sacrifice.

The old paganism was tenacious of life. Brigantia, the ancient goddess of the Brigantes (a fire goddess) became St. Bride in Scotland and she appears in Llansanffraid = Church of St. Bride in Wales, whence she was carried by Irish settlers. Significantly her Islay site is Kilbride, only a stone's throw from Pàirc Bhaile Néill with its fire and fertility associations. Similarly, nemeton, a holy place appears in the Firth of Clyde as Roseneath—the Promontory of the Nemeton (the old church is well worth a visit) and in Islay we have Ardnave (as in Knave). Now there are on record some four Irish saints called Nem and, as it stands, this name commemorates one of them but it may well conceal an older Aird Neimhidh = Temple Height.

During the late 17th century the Presbytery of Gareloch had to discipline certain gentlemen who, during a time of trouble locally, had repaired to the ancient religious settlement of Maolrubha on an island on Loch Maree, (Maol Rubha's loch), and there offered sacrifice of a horse to the god "Maorie". The "god" in question was the saint Maol Rubha (O.I. Mailrubai)—The Tonsured Ruddy One.

Maol Rubha came from Bangor in the North of Ireland about 671 and founded an abbey at Applecross. He died in 722 at an advanced age. Several daughter houses of Applecross were established and, in Islay, we have Kilarrow =Cille Mhaoil Rubha at Bridgend—once the main church of the island. Maol Rubha is a saint with one foot in the Christian world and one in the pagan as his name shows. Islay has, in fact a large number of early churches but we will deal with them in a later chapter. Meanwhile we will deal with some other old names.

27

The Book of Genesis Ch. 31 vv 44–55 describes the construction of a site of the Baile Néill—type—except that the "mount" in this case is artificial as in one or two mainland sites in Scotland. The pillar is erected first and then the stones are heaped up to make the "mount". When the "mount is completed it is hallowed by a sacrifice and the participants take part in a solemn feast. The writer is very vague as to the precise significance except that it concerns the patriarch Jacob, his father-in-law Laben and the daughters of Laben—i.e. it is of sexual significance. One good example of this artificial "mount" type can be seen at the head of Loch Craignish.

Our Oldest Names

Islay: This is a convenient time to deal with the name Islay itself as it is not unconnected with the ancient gods. First and foremost we must point out that the name occurs twice in Scotland: as the name of a river and as the name of an island. Rivers usually have feminine names, being, in fact, ancient goddesses of fertility. It is hardly surprising to find that we talk too of Ile Ghorm (feminine) and Fheòir, Green grassy Islay. Again, it is surely more than co-incidence that the Isla River marks off the north of the ancient province of Angus and Angus was the inheritor of Islay, when first the Scots came to the land.

If we want proof that Islay is a goddess, we find it in the name Bruide mac Derilei ri Cruithintuathi—Brude son of Der-ile, King of Pictland, who died in 706 A.D. Der-ile means Daughter of the Islay (we recall that among the Picts succession lay through the female) and here is a typical pagan type name which we could compare with such names as Dionysius = Born of Dionysus, Morgan = Born of the Sea, MacCodrum = Son of the Good Serpent and so on. As we will see, Islay was a religious centre in early times. The earliest dateable reference to the island is in Adomnan's biography of Columba where he speaks of a certain rascal as "Feredach . . . qui in Ilea insula habitabat". According to Adomnan, Ile (i.e. the island) is a feminine -A or -IA stem but unfortunately there is little evidence by which we could assess the corresponding river name. It is worth noting that Ilea stands in apposition to insula, and the -a is the Latin noun ending and not an adjectival termination.

The next reference is in the Annals of Ulster where we find this entry under the year 740:—Terra motus in Ili (dative, gender doubtful) = Earth-quake in Islay. In 1095 there is a mention of "insula quae vocatur Yle" where Yle is again feminine. From then on it is commonly, Ila, Yla and later Ilay. By the 19th century it has become Isla and Islay. The modern Gaelic is Ile (ee-le).

The late Professor Watson referred the name to a Gaulish word meaning a flank, and this is far from impossible. The Flanked Island and the Flanking river would be reasonable, but the word in question is uncommon and appears to be masculine or neuter.

Recently a gallant attempt has been made to explain it as I-lagha = The Island of the Bended Bow. This is an attractive theory but there are some objections to it:—

(1) The word "i" meaning an island is rare. It may not be just a borrowing from Norse, but it cannot be the element in Islay (river).

(2) There is no evidence known to me of "Islay" ever having been written with a -g- though in the seventh century, when we have our earliest references, the -g- should have been audible in pronunciation.

(3) "Lagh" (literally "law" and cognate with "lex") means, in this sense, not so much the bow itself as the stretch or character of the bow.

It remains safest to say that we do not know what Islay means but we will pass on now to examine some other ancient names.

The Irish manuscript, Accalamh Fir nAlbann, gives the following information:—

"Is iad a randsaide orba inile".—

Aengus beag dan mac Eirc unum filium habuit .i. Muredac

Cet treb inile. (These are the settlements in Islay):—

Odeich XX tech (cf. Adomnan 64a)

Freag C tech (or CXX tech)

Cladrois LX tech

Ros Deorand XXX tech

Ard Bes XXX tech

Loichrois XXX tech

Aitha cassil XXX tech

Cinel Aengusa XXX tech Caillnae acht isbeca na feranna taighe Cenel n-Aengusa. i fer trichot".

This statement reflects the conditions in Islay in the days of the Scottish Dal Riada, when Islay was given to Aonghus Beag of the sons of Erc. It would appear that Aonghus himself took only one small part of the island and that it was really Muredach, his son and his descendents who took possession.

Can these places named in the list be pinned down to-day? Many attempts have been made, some good, some not so good. One which is unlikely to be correct, tells us that Ros Deorand is really the south end of Jura. In point of fact, Jura is a Norse name given some hundreds of years after this list was drawn up. These names are not really so very difficult but the first thing to realise is that they are not given in the ordinary Nominative forms: they are all Dative-Locative except Caillnae which is Genitive. Freag and Ard Bes look like Nominatives and may, in fact, be errors—Freag almost certainly is.

Having mentioned Freag, let us deal with it. This place has very obviously been the "metropolis"—it has about twice the number of houses that the next biggest place has. It seems reasonable, therefore, to look for it in that part of the island which served as a centre for business in ancient times and we find that, until Bowmore was built in the eighteenth century, the business centre was Bridgend, the geographical heart of the island. Now, if we turn to the old rent-rolls, we find that, in the 1686 roll, the name Dall Ochdamh na Freighe appears and its position in the list shows that the modern farm of Daill is meant. It would appear from this that Daill, which lies just behind Bridgend, was one eighth (ochdamh) of Freag, and Octovullin, lying almost adjacent was, we may assume, another eighth. They are separated now-a-days by an intrusive Norse farm. Here we may mention that for a farm to be " an eighth" was very common in Mediaeval times in the Highlands, but that is another story.

We may take it, then, that Freag is the ancient name for Kilarrow Parish and before anyone takes a map and points out that Daill is not an eighth of Kilarrow, let me remind him that this is a measure of produce, not of extent. Further, we have no way of telling how much of the present parish was actually occupied by the Gaels and how much was still in the hands of the aboriginal population.

Next in the list comes Cladrois. Ros is a promontory, so we need look nowhere except at promontories. Near Port na haven is the small hill and settlement of Cladville and the "ville" is just the Norse word "fjall", a hill— this area was almost entirely Norse-speaking at a rather later date, but several ancient names were preserved because the Norse retained them. Further, the Rent Roll lists Octocladsel with Octofad. What the "sel" part may mean I do not know but the "clad" is clear enough. Cladrois is, then the southern part of the Rhinns, the modern Kilchiaran Parish. As to what the "clad" means, it would appear to be connected with "calad"—having some such meaning as "hard" or "rough" and this describes the most exposed part of the island quite well.

Let us now take Lochrois, the Loch of the Promontory, and surely this can only be the Loch Gorm area. In other words, this is the modern Kilchoman Parish, or at least, that part of it lying around the loch.

Ros Deorand would appear to mean the Pilgrim's Promontory and I think this must be Ardnave. My reasons are as follows:—

(1) It is the only suitable "ros" remaining.
(2) It was, apparently, anciently a parish in its own right although now a part of Kilchoman.
(3) The "nave" is not, as generally stated, "naomh" = Holy. Speakers of Gaelic pronounce it like the English "nave"—a sound totally different from that of "naomh". In point of fact this may be the pre-Christian name for a religious building, "nemeton", (the word we find in Roseneath), though St. Nemh is probable. This was certainly a place of pilgrimage.

Aitha cassil is also fairly straight-forward. At the tip of the Oa there is an ancient fort known as Dùn Athad and "dùn" is, of course, the old word for a fortified place, a cashel or castle. Aitha cassil is, as it says, the Atha Castle, the Oa Castle. The change in the vowels of Atha was caused by Norse influence. At the entrance, if one can call it that, to the Oa, at Cragabus Farm, there is an ancient and sadly-despoiled burial mound. The Norse took the word "atha" to be a mis-pronunciation of their word "haugr", a burial mound, hence Oa. (Gaelic Ogh).

We can now deal with Odeich, and this is a most interesting one. A certain bishop, setting out from Iona to return to Ireland after paying a visit to St. Columba, was so careless as to leave his bachull, or pastoral staff, behind, but putting ashore at the small island of Aithche, near Islay, he found that the staff had been miraculously removed from Iona to this place, and, lo and behold, there it was lying on the grass in front of him! The island where this rather

30

improbable miracle took place is generally agreed to have been Texa, near Port Ellen, and the point in telling this story is that Aithche and Odeich are the same word, they both come from "adaig". This looks like the word meaning "night" though why anyone should want to call a place Night is not at all clear to me. I should guess that the name is religious, in origin; this was a place of fire and fertility cults. Odeich is the Port Ellen area, which in earlier days, was probably the Parish of Kilbride.

We are left now with only one name in the main list, Ard Bes, and the Caillnae of the Cinel Aengus and we have two sections of the island left to fit them into, viz. Kilmeny Parish and the section of Kildalton Parish called Lanndaidh, which is that section from Allt a' Chrochaire at Loch Knock to Proaig.

To take Ard Bes first, I do not know what "bes" may mean, but I suggest that this "Height of Bes" may be the dùn crowned by what appears to be a broch with a mediaeval structure on top of that, known variously by the Norse name Dùn Bhoreraig or the pre-Norse (and indeed, pre-Gaelic) name, Dùn Lossit. This dùn lies in the very heart of Kilmeny Parish. I have found two tiny clues which may be considered to strengthen this conjecture: it seems that an old name in this district, and used apparently for the district was Ard Nis. It seems just possible that "bes" is a mistake for "nes". If this is so, and if you want to know what "nes" means, I can only suggest that you look round for someone who can tell you what the other (Loch, etc.) Nes(s) means—I do not know. The Norse too help us a little here. They did not adopt the "bes" or "nes" but they did call the Parish of Kilmeny "The Heights" (Na Hearradh in Gaelic) and this name is still in use locally as a name for the parish.

We are now forced to believe that Caillnae was the Lanndaidh, although the two names cannot possibly be connected.

Is there any evidence at all of this? We must confess that there is very little, though we may mention the following:—

(1) This is a poor, infertile area as we are told Caillnae was. It is also the part lying nearest to the part of the Mainland from which we may assume Aonghus to have come.

(2) The name appears to be connected with "coll", a hazel tree, and this area was well-wooded until quite recent times with hazel as one of the commonest trees.

(3) Local memory, which can be surprisingly reliable, points to this eastern part of the Parish as the true, ancient part and it is worth noticing that when, about the 16th century, the number of churches was reduced, the people chose to retain the church in the Lanndaidh as the church for the whole of this part of the island. Although this church was in such an incredibly inconvenient place, it was not till well on in the 18th century that it was finally abandoned and a new church built in a more suitable part of the parish.

31

As regards population figures, while it is, of course, impossible to give exact numbers with the information at our disposal, we can get a rough idea.

We have in the Accalamh list a total of 330 houses with the additional information that the thirty houses of Caillnae produced thirty men for the armed muster. I worked out averages for several groups of Islay homes and found that they worked out at something between three and four people per house. As the ancient family was patriarchal, probably the average per house would be rather higher, say five. This would give us a total, for the free population with, say, a third extra for various bondmen, slaves, aboriginals and the like, of about 2,200 for the 6th–7th centuries of the Christian Era. This seems a reasonable number.

It is possible to take our population figures just a little further.

On top of this figure of 2,000 plus, we have a number of Norse settlers to reckon with from about 800 on. Their numbers are harder to estimate, but there are altogether some 80 Norse farm names—admittedly some of these are very late, so let's allow 50 for the areas of primary settlement. If we reckon eight to ten people per farm—which seems to compare fairly well with Norse farms elsewhere. we can reckon a Norse population of some 500–600 by about 1000 A.D., rising to perhaps a thousand by 1266. This would give a total population of something like 3,500 in 1266 if we assume that the coming of the Norse retarded the rate of increase of the Gaelic population.

This figure agrees reasonably well with Hayes-McCoy's estimate of 4,000–4,500 during the 15th century.[1] It also agrees reasonably well with the estimated doubling of the world's population between the time of Christ and the year 1600.

[1] Hayes-MacCoy, Scots Mercenaries in Ireland.

CHAPTER 4

NA DUIN — DEFENSIVE POINTS

Wherever the word "dùn" or "dyn" (its Welsh form) appears, one may be sure that the Celt has passed that way. London, Verdun, Dumbarton, Dunkeld and so to Edinburgh which is Dùn Eideann in Gaelic: Dynas Edyn is the earlier form, reminding us that those parts once belonged to the Cymrian Votadini with whom King Arthur is associated (cf. Arthur's Seat—Suidhe Artuir) and of course, it has no connection with the Northumbrian Edwin.

A dùn is a fort, normally one on a hill—Dunoon, (-oon of unknown meaning), is a good example of one.

In bye-gone days a hill fort was a very useful thing and lucky the man who possessed one—such a person was "raitheil" from "rath", a circle. Such a man could dwell in safety within his "rath" (the word "rath" is found in Islay at The Raw, an old smithy near Bridgend, but probably Carraig an Ratha, near MacArthur's Head is just the Lucky Headland, where you get a lot of fish).

Islay has literally dozens of ancient forts ranging from the very simple and primitive one near Lossit in the Rhinns, where the "fort" is no more than a little headland fenced off by a crazy wall of dry stones with an entry at the steepest and most dangerous point, to sophisticated structures such as Nòsbrig, built by a skilled engineer. And, of course, the range in dates must likewise be enormous but, alas, we can do little more than guess at these dates. Further, although attempts have been made to identify certain forts as the dwellings of specific historical characters, for our purposes we can ignore this and concentrate on the different types of fort and their names.

(1) The first type to be considered is not, strictly speaking, a fort at all, but as the dùns are descended from it, it is worth noting. Bronze Age man, the herder, had to be reasonably mobile—he had to go where there was grass and where there was no stronger Bronze Age man! During this period tents came into use; the height of luxury at the time (cf. Genesis, ch. 13). Tents were normally made wig-wam style as being the most convenient shape; you simply had to stick a pole in the ground and drape a large skin blanket over it. Later, when improvements in agricultural method had made it possible to settle down in one place, at least for the winter, it became the custom to build a "tent" of stone, circular of course, and, some at least maintain, use the original skin tent as a roof. Many of these "hut" circles can be seen in Islay but no names for these early villages have survived. There is perhaps a

C

cluster of them, only excavation could tell us this for certain, by the roadside above Bruthach Sheònis and an isolated one near the mouth of the Kintour River.

(2) As people gained more worldly goods, the question of protection from robbers arose and, as locks and bars and even strong towers were unavailable, other means of protection had to be found. Three possibilities presented themselves:—

(a) A little knob of rock, steep on at least three sides, would be difficult for the enemy to approach unseen and, while he was climbing up, he would be at the mercy of the defenders. Such little "dùin", large enough for only one patriarchal family, are perhaps Islay's most common type. Dùn Fhinn, Dùn Mideir, Dùnan Charmaic, etc. (Notice that these bear Gaelic names.)

(b) A headland or a cliff could be fenced off and utilised in the same way as an enemy could approach from only one side. This sort is found near Lossit in the Rhinns, and in the truly magnificent fort of Dùn Athad in the Oa, which must have been virtually impregnable.

(c) Again, though not strictly a dùn, but serving the same purpose, is the islet. There are examples of defended islets on Loch Lossit, Loch Gorm and, best known of all, Loch Finlaggan, which eventually became the capital of the Lordship of the Isles. Although the existing visible ruins on these islets are relatively late, beyond doubt, there are traces of primitive man underneath.

Where no suitable islet existed, it was often possible to construct one by towing a raft to the spot selected, fixing it in position with piers and piling it with stones and turf until it was securely anchored to the lake floor. Such artificial islands are called crannogs, and they are found throughout the Celtic areas from Switzerland to Lewis. An example is visible in the glen between Bealach Askaig and Loch Aluinn where it has been exposed by the partial draining of the loch. In this case the main beams are of pine and would suggest that there were rather more large trees in these days than there are now on the island. Other probable sites are in Loch Skerrols, Loch Bharradail and Loch nan Gial. The name of no crannog has survived.

(3) Types (b) and (c) above lead on to the next type because these, like the crannog, really need many hands to build and maintain. Corporate activities, in other words, beginning to displace the old, basic Law of Survival, "Every one for himself". The Iron Age had arrived. Although we have no written records, we can picture some strong-willed people coming to the fore among a cluster of families and setting to, to organise and direct the united efforts of the people to food production and defence. An area could now be marked off as "Our Land" and its borders could be policed (notice however that this is not "patriotism" in our sense. It is "us", not "our country" which is important.) In the event of danger threatening,

weaker members of the community, cattle and goods could be taken into the central defensive point, nearly always a hill, and this could be defended until the enemy got tired and went away again.

As before, these forts are of various sorts:—

(a) Dûn Bhorrochill Mór (two similar forts of the name) represents the simplest type—a straggling, irregular wall of dry stone running round a plateau. Since the name Borrochill is not Gaelic, it seems reasonable to assume that it is Cruthnean (Pictish) and that these forts had already been built and indeed were in occupation when the Gaelic speakers arrived. (The name appears to be uchell—high, the word we get in the Ochil Hills, prefixed by an intensive = very. The qualifying adjective is, of course, just the Gaelic, "great".) In all probability the Kildalton Borrochill became the centre of the area called Oidech and the other of the Kilchoman area. This would account for the names having been preserved, just as the Jebusite name "Jerusalem" was preserved by the Israelites when they took the city.

(b) Very different in construction is Nòsbrig, a neat, rectangular fort of turf and stone which looks rather like a scale model of Maiden Castle, Dorset, except that it is a perfect rectangle.

It is matched by Dún Ghuthaire, a short way off, which is very similar except that in this case we have a D–shape! Could these possibly be Cymrian in origin? Only excavation can tell, but if they are, many theories will be upset. Much more likely they are relatively late and represent an attempt by the Norse to control the two main routes between Port Askaig and Lochindaal. The former controls the "Glen Road" while the latter overshadows the main road. It is perhaps significant that both bear Norse names. If this was their object, they certainly failed miserably as no record of activities from within these walls survives either in tradition or on paper.

(c) Different in design and conception is Lossit in Kilmeny, which appears to be a broch, though it is so dilapidated that excavation would be needed to confirm this. Since it is so different from the other Lossit, it seems a fair conjecture that this elaborate structure was erected on top of an earlier one, retaining the name, The name is in fact very ancient indeed, being among the earliest types of Indo-European name found in Britain. It is related to such words as Lovat and the like. Meaning is uncertain.

In spite of a great deal of work having been done, the origins of the brochs remain obscure, but the main facts are simple enough.

About the beginning of the Christian Era or a little earlier, the people of the northern part of Scotland developed an entirely new and unique type of fort. Circular, fairly small in diameter, it resembled a huge thimble. The walls of dry stone were thick enough to contain chambers and passages. The entry was a low, narrow passage with a guardroom opening off it. Some brochs have a handy water-supply either inside or nearby (ours has one fairly close), others were less well-favoured.

Apparently the broch-builders were seized by the urge to travel, and two main lines of migration, one down the East Coast, stopping just short of the English border and the other down the West Coast, zig-zagging from mainland to islands and back right down to Galloway, can be traced.

Nothing is known for sure about the people of the brochs. It would seem likely that the broch was developed by some genius who got the idea of extending the walls of a circular dùn upwards though, at present, the influence of foreign ideas or invaders cannot be discounted. Early Irish writings speak of a terrible race of pirates whom they called Fomorians—the name seems to mean "People from below the Sea (i.e. horizon)" and it is conjectured that these are our broch-builders. At any rate, these Fomorians disappear as suddenly as they appeared leaving no clue as to their looks, language or anything else. Possibly the expedition of Constantius Chlorus to the Orkneys in 297 A.D. had something to do with their disappearance.

Islay's broch has an excellent position, commanding a view of the sea on all sides and yet with easy access to a harbour on the Sound of Islay which still bears the Norse name—Borreraig—Fort Harbour. In other words fort and harbour were still in use as a unit when the Norse arrived, though by that time it had almost certainly become the centre of Gaelic-speaking Ard Bes.

(4) Lastly we might mention another and an enigmatic type of fort: the vitrified fort. These originate on the Continent and it was once believed that they were associated with Celts, but recent excavation has suggested that they may well be a lot older than was previously thought and indeed the Islay examples do not appear to have belonged to Indo-Europeans.

These forts were built of stone, tied with wooden beams and, if accident or enemy action set them on fire, the heat generated might be sufficient to fuse or "vitrify" the stone. East Coast examples resemble the Continental forts, being rectangular and fairly large, but West Coast examples are small and circular. These forts occur here and there throughout Argyll, but Islay has a whole line of them running down the east coast and here and there at other points on the coast. They are tiny places, each on a knoll of rock, each with a tiny harbour and each showing signs of systematic destruction. These forts were evidently built by a people of unknown language: not one of the forts preserves its own name but is simply "An Dùn". Possible exceptions are Trudernish, which looks like Norse, but is actually of unknown meaning and Dunnyveg or (better) Dùn Naomhaig (the Mediaeval castle is almost certainly on the site of one of them), where the various explanations given of the name are all, for one reason or another, unsatisfactory.[1]

These poor folk of the vitrified forts, whoever they may have been came to Islay as settlers trying to wrest a living from the sea. They were not made welcome and to-day only the pathetic ruined homes remain still showing traces of the flames which destroyed them and their occupants.

It cannot be too strongly stressed that the above is merely a rough classification of the various types of dùn and bears no relation to their ages. Then again there are many dùns which it is hard to fit into any of the above categories e.g.

Dùn a' Mhullaich Bhàin in Kildalton. Much work is needed in this field. It is also to be remembered that the name of a dùn does not, in itself, associate it with any known historical person. Thus Dùnan Charmaic is unlikely to have been the dwelling-place of Carmac, High King of Ireland and it is to be questioned if the legendary (and mythological) hero Fionn lived at Dùn Fhinn.

Here is a brief summary of the probable builders:—

(1) The vitrified forts were built by an unknown people on the verge of extinction.
(2) The brochs were built by an unknown people who came from the North of Scotland.
(3) The neat, well-planned forts may just possibly be the work of some branch of the Cymbrians, but are more likely to be Norse.
(4) The large, straggling forts were probably the work of Cruithneans or of people subject to them, but were taken over by the conquering Gaelic-speakers.
(5) The small, circular forts, and probably the crannogs are the work of Gaelic-speaking settlers from Ireland. Since they are of Gaelic origin they bear Gaelic names.

Here are some "dùn" names:—

Kildalton Parish

Dùn Fhinn:	Presumably called after the Irish hero Fionn Mac Coul. This personage stands on the border-line between history and mythology (cf. O'Rahilly: Early Irish History and Mythology).
Dún a' Mhullaich Bhàin	Fort of the Fair Summit.
Dún Bhorrochill Mhóir:	Borrochill Mór, various spellings. Apparently the Old Celtic adjective uchell (uxellos = high) used as a noun with an intensive prefix cf. Ochil Hills.
Dunnyveg:	Meaning doubtful. Dwelly lists words which nearly (but not quite) match, with the meaning "ship" presumably borrowings from the Latin "navis". The one most favoured is "naimheag", given as a little ship and this would make good sense but—
	(1) This is not the way the name is actually pronounced locally and literary sources testify to the present-day pronunciation's being used at least as early as the 15th century.
	(2) The word "naimheag" does not occur, as far as I know, in Irish, (Dineen gives "naoi", naomhog=a canoe). It is, therefore, a rather rare dialect form.
	Unfortunately, Dwelly does not tell us where he got the word.

37

Again it has been suggested that the Dùn contains the name of the saint of Kilmonivaig, but the local pronunciation refuses to co-operate. Were it a saint's name one would have expected to find that saint's cell nearby but there is no sign or memory of one nor, is there any certain trace of a chapel within the building.

Kilarrow Parish

Dùn Bhruichlinn: Probably the centre of the district called Freag. The name appears to contain a commemoration of Bricriu, God of the Underworld and this name was certainly not given with the sanction of Columba!

Dùn Nòsbrig: A rectangular turf and stone structure bearing only a relatively late Norse name: Knaus borg—Rocky hill Fort.

Kilmeny Parish

Dùn Chollapus: A fort of the small, late type but the name is a puzzle. Is it a lost Norse farm (bólstaðr)? No such name occurs in any of the farm lists and it is hard to believe that the adjacent land was ever cultivated as it is either peat or thin gravelly soil over-lying quartzite. It may be Koll's farm but I have no other suggestion and Koll could have been either Norse or a Norse-speaking Scot, Colla.

Dún Ghuaire: (Ghuthaire with a hiatus between the syllables) it is tempting to see here the old Gaelic "guaire"—noble (as in MacGuire, MacQuarry, Hardy etc.) but it is hard to reconcile this with the local pronunciation. The name has survived also in the adjacent form of Airidh Ghuthairidh. The authorities explain this as "sheiling of Godfrey's", sheiling—whatever that may mean, but it is, of course, the sheiling attached to Dùn Ghutharaidh.

Locally it is believed that the name is indeed an affectionate form of Godred or Godfrey and that the man in question was a MacNeill. The Islay MacNeills did claim a Norse ancestry so, as stated above, this fort, like its companion, Nòsbrig, may be Norse.

Dùn Lossit: The probable broch. It has been reconstructed in Mediaeval times apparently as a look-out. There are traces of at least one vallum guarding the approaches to the hill and the route to the harbour is fairly easy to follow. The name is ancient.

Rhinns

Borrachill Mór: (various spellings) Rather like the fort of similar name at Kildalton. Probably the centre of the Loch Rois area.

Dùn Mideir: A small, circular fort. Mideir was the attendant on the Goddess Greine of the Tuatha Dé Danann, one of the early peoples of Ireland. There is also the word "miadar"—a meadow but it is unlikely that this word could become Mideir.

Dùn Glas an   Another small fort. The Grey Fort on the Green Meadow.
  Lòin Ghuirm:

Dùn nan Nighean: Maiden Fort. On the sea-coast. Said to be the place where the local chief kept his daughters for safety.

Dùn Lossit: See Kilmeny. This is a very primitive type of stronghold but may well have been the centre of the district of Cladrois.

There are dùns of the vitrified fort type at Octofad and nearer Portnahaven.

Oa
Dùn Athad: As mentioned elsewhere, Dùn Add (monosyllable) is the oldest capital of the Scots in Scotland. It is hard to believe that the two names are unconnected. This is the genitive singular of a dental stem of unknown meaning.

There may well have been a tribal connection between Jura, Islay and the Crinan area. They do form a natural unit. Unfortunately we do not have any way of proving this at present. At the time of the invasion of the sons of Erc the dominant tribe in Kintyre was the Epidii, the People of the Horse—old Irish tales recount raids on them and talk of their leader Echde Echbel (horse mouth) whose daughter was stolen away during a raid on (probably) Dunaverty. These are the ancestors of the MacEacherns. Now animal totem names are found fairly commonly in the Cruithean areas of both Ireland and Scotland; they are rare or unknown among the other groups, so we can assume that the Epidii were Pictish.[2]

In later times the MacEacherns are found in the Craignish area, having been, no doubt, displaced northwards at a fairly early date, probably even before the main invasion at Crinan. The name Bellanoch may well hold a memory of their former northern border for it means "The End of the Horse Ford". Tradition, probably based on fact, tells that one MacEachern persuaded an heiress of Machrihanish to elope with him and the couple fled to Islay. All the Islay MacEacherns are said to be descended from that couple and, indeed, in Islay they are known as Clann an Ilich. The Children of the Islayman. The girl was one of seven daughters who owned seven white horses—a typical folk-tale motif.

One other slender clue to another tribal name of South Argyll is known to me: the Cymbrian name, (Ben) Arthur. Its name and its position suggest that there may have been a tribe called the Artures, or something of the like, an off-shoot of the Strathclyde Britons pushing its way into the county. If they reached Islay—and the name MacArthur is found anciently in Islay though it was by no means common, then this might account for our Cymbrian-looking dùns. Much work with the spade remains to be done!

39

Eacharnach, an abandoned steading in the remote area between Kildalton and Kilmeny simply means Horse Park, but, as a form name it is unusual. It may just possibly mark a place once occupied by these "People of the Horse" though our earliest traditions of the Islay MacEacherns place them in Crosprig and Coul.

[1] Recently I have been given the name Dùn nan Gall—Foreigners' Fort for the vitrified fort near Proaig.
[2] Ptolemy of Alexandria (fl. circa 130 A.D.) gives Epidion Akron as the name of Kintyre and, from the Irish sources, we know that its name locally was Aird Echde, with the same meeting, Horse Promontory. The Irish stories seem to preserve a memory of a time when the "Horse Tribe" occupied Man also.

CHAPTER 5

THE EARLY CHURCH

On August 24th 410 A.D. the Goths, under their leader Alaric, stormed the Salarian Gate and burst into Rome. Truly men might have said that day, "The lights are going out all over Europe, and Asia, and Africa."

Actually not much happened immediately. The hooligans spent some three days roaming the streets and gathering portable loot, then off they went again, leaving the City looking much as usual, with its people rather shaken and worried but quite unhurt, for these Goths appear to have acted with great moderation. The significance of that week was that a spark had been ignited which would bring down in flames the greatest political entity this world has ever known. The British Empire rested on Respect, the respect that lesser breeds should feel towards the Imperial Race; the Roman Empire rested on Invincibility, Rome could never be defeated. In both cases, once the bubble burst, the end was inevitable. The fall of Rome was sad, but much worse was to follow, namely, an outburst of anarchy, cruelty, misery and oppression throughout Europe, seldom, if ever, paralleled in this world's sad history. The utter chaos which followed the collapse of the imperial organisation was to last for, quite literally, hundreds of years and, indeed, to this day no power has arisen to fill the vacuum left by the fall of Rome.

After 410, the disorganised civil service failed to provide the regular supplies on which the armed forces depended. The frontier guards deserted and proceeded to ravage the very lands they had been paid to defend. Self-styled "emperors" appeared and proceeded to savage each other, using the promise of boundless loot to gain the allegiance of the Legions. And while they were all busy quarrelling, the barbarians moved in. As no central authority existed to drive them out again they came, they saw and they stayed. They chased farmers from their steadings, they chased merchants from their fine villas, they lit cooking fires on priceless mosaic floors, stoking them up with antique furniture, they looted, they tortured, they killed. Year after year this continued and then, just when it seemed that the barbarians, sated with their orgies of destruction, were beginning to settle down and leave folk in peace, another even worse horror burst upon the world, one aimed at men's souls.

The Prophet Mahommed died about 632, leaving as a legacy a large following of fanatics. Quarrelsome they undoubtedly were, indeed schism had reared its ugly head within months of their leader's death when a large body of his followers broke off from the "official" leadership to follow the Prophet's

41

daughter Fatima and her husband Ali—the Shia Muslims. On one issue only were all Muslims united: viz. the world must be saved from error—by force. Now these were no ignorant fuzzie-wuzzies like the last lot; these were people with a level of culture sufficiently high for them to be able to look with contempt upon the benighted Christians and they were thus prepared to treat these exactly as the whites of a later date were to treat the African negro.

In 634 the Muslims crossed the Jordan. In 635 they were in Damascus. Two years later saw Jerusalem and the Holy Land in Muslim hands and in 641 Egypt fell to them. Another sixty years of slaughter and misery brought down the old North African provinces, Libya, Cirenaica, Tripoli, Mauretania. And worse was to come. In 711 Gibraltar fell and one more generation saw all Iberia gone with the Muslims streaming across the plains of Gaul. Mercifully Charles Martell was able to dam the flood at Poitiers. We who talk of the strain of modern life do not know what strain means! The Muslims were at last driven out of Spain in the year Columbus discovered America and it was Bonnie Prince Charlie's grandfather who finally turned them away eastwards from Vienna.

Britannia, the brightest gem in the Imperial Crown, suffered the most awful anguish as the Empire slowly crumbled. Unlike the Continental Empire, Britannia escaped the Muslim menace but that is all one can say.

Amidst all this turmoil only one part of civilised Europe escaped—Ireland.

Ireland became the Land of Promise, the Haven of Peace, the Scholars' Paradise. Ireland had never been in the Empire and it suffered none of the agonies of its collapse. Ireland was not, however, the Land of Perfection; rather it was the Land of Anomalies. The Irish were noted for the richness of their lands, the general poverty and meanness of their buildings, their old-fashioned system of government and their Iron Age way of life. An Irish chief might have visited the great cities of the Continent and even Rome itself. He might possess a library suitable to a man of culture and refinement. He might festoon his wife with jewellery of the most beautiful and sophisticated sort. Yet that same man was quite prepared to live in a filthy mud hut and eat his dinner out the pot while squatting on the floor!

Ireland was, in fact, a land on the borderline between kingdom and tribal territory. A large number of petty kings, really tribal chiefs, each living in his circular "rath" or fortress (cf. The Raw, an old smithy near Bridgend) was supposed to owe some sort of allegiance to a vast and complicated hierarchy of overlords of all sorts, the top of the pyramid being, in theory at least, the High King (Ard-rígh Eireann) whose headquarters were at Tara, Co. Meath (Teamhair nan Rígh).

Like ancient Greece, Ireland possesses a "heroic" literature which has received great publicity in recent years. This literature tells of the days when a large and powerful Ulster, centred on Emain Macha (Navan Fort near Armagh) lived in a state of endemic warfare with the rest of Ireland. Ulster was able to keep her end up because she was helped by a "good guy", Cuchullin, who may be loosely compared to Hector in the Iliad.

As in the case of Greece, when the curtain rises on the actual historical stage, the reality is very different and the intervening space can be filled in only

42

by guesswork. By the beginning of the historic period the old, large Ulster is gone; divided into three kingdoms:—Aileach, the eastern counties; Oriel, the central section, and Ulster, Donegal and the West of the present Northern Ireland. By this time there were two main power groupings in Ireland: north and south with the northern branch of the O'Neill family being, by and large, the most influential force in the land. (Columba himself was of this family).

There are records of Christianity in Ireland at a very early date, but the first serious mission appears to have been that of Palladius, who was sent by Pope Celestine about 431. His work appears to have aroused a scattered but quite satisfactory interest in the South, but it was the "unofficial" mission of the more practical Patrick to the North and Midlands that triggered off the chain reaction which drove out the ancient gods. Starting from the basic principle that the best people to keep in with are those most influential, Patrick appears to have decided to win over the leading Ulster families, including, of course, the O'Neills, and this worldly policy paid handsome dividends. Patrick may not have driven out the serpents but he certainly drove out the druids!

Who was this Patrick? His dates have been the subject of bitter argument and all we can usefully say here is that he lived during the fifth century— probably slightly later than Palladius. His place of birth has also been forgotten and the learned have wasted much time arguing about where he was born. Certainty is impossible: the information he himself gives is too vague, but the most probable location is the area east of Dumbarton. He was carried off from a town called Bannavea Tabernae during a slave-raid and he worked as a slave in Ireland for six years, during which time he mastered the Irish tongue.

Bannavea Tabernae appears to have been a Roman type settlement and Patrick's father was a deacon in the local Christian Church. Now, of course, the Romans' short occupation of Southern Scotland ended centuries before Patrick was born and it does seem amazing that there should have been a settlement of this sort in existence as late as Patrick's time but it is not, of course, impossible. How strong was Roman influence north of Hadrian's Wall? Probably entirely non-existent north of the Highland Line and it would appear doubtful if there could be much in the Lennox, Patrick's birthplace in Scottish tradition. Excavation has proved the existence of a village at the west end of the old Antonine Wall at the point where it meets the Clyde. This is in Old Kilpatrick Parish, which just means Parish of Patrick's Church and the sacred well, St. Patrick's Well can be seen to this day. Was it in, or near this village, on a spot buried beneath 19th century tenements that this great man was born? Was it during Nati's raid on Strathclyde that he was carried off? We will probably never know for certain. By the way, his name is Latin, Patricius, meaning Noble. When he went to Ireland he found that people there had difficulty in pronouncing the letter -p- and he became known as Cothraige.

Patrick himself tells of his flight from slavery and of how he made his way to the coast where he found a ship sailing for Gaul (France). He reached Gaul safely only to find that there had recently been a big Teutonic raid on the area and he almost died of hunger. Finally he re-joined his family but found himself unable to settle. After a spell of training he returned to Ireland, apparently after some sort of disagreement with the Church "establishment".

Patrick is known as the Patron Saint of Ireland. More fittingly he might be known as the Patron Saint of Europe for, as we have seen, Patrick's Ireland was the only bastion which did not fall to the barbarian or the Muslim; the centre from which civilisation was to flow back to the Continent.

It is often said that the Irish Church was "different" from the Continental Church and so, in fact, it was, but it is important to understand wherein the differences lay. First and foremost, the Irish Church did not differ widely in doctrinal concepts from the rest of the Western Church. It was, in no sense, a "Protestant" Church in the present-day understanding of the term and, like the rest of Western Europe, it looked to Rome for guidance—though it was quite prepared to question Rome's decisions. Rather it was in the matter of organisation that the Church in Ireland differed. The Christianity of the Continent, developed over the past few hundred years was based on the town where the local leader—the bishop—had his seat and administered the landward areas through the lesser clergy. Since, during a period of instability, the town was the only place affording reasonable security, the place to which everyone must be prepared to flee in time of trouble, this was the obvious and the sensible way in which to organise things. This was the type of Church which Patrick probably envisaged for Ireland but really it was quite inappropriate there since Ireland possessed no towns. In Ireland the population was spread fairly evenly over the habitable land and the country had enjoyed relatively peaceful conditions for generations (fighting was common, but it was the fighting born of natural roughness rather than the calculated slaughter of war). In these circumstances the Church which grew up in Ireland could only be a mirror-image of the secular conditions existing there. It could consist only of copies of the petty-king's household, raths, havens of God, little communities dedicated to His service—in a word, monasteries.

The idea of the religious community seems to have originated in Egypt and there is some evidence to show that this Eastern concept did influence Irish thinking but, be that as it may, there sprang up in Ireland a very large number of little monasteries, each ruled over by an abbot, or "father" who stood in the same relationship to his "sons" as the Christian God stands to us. This is the sort of community of which we read in the lives of the Irish saints. The bishop was indeed a recognised figure but, far from being the sophisticated administrator known on the Continent, he was rather an especially holy sort of clergyman to whom lesser men—and even the great Columba himself—deferred. As time passed two monasteries, or groups of monasteries came to predominate: Clonmacnois, founded by Ciaran, and Derry/Durrow/Iona founded by Columba and to some extent the lesser houses tended to fall into line with one or other of those. These monasteries were very different from the Benedictine or Cistercian houses of the Middle Ages. An Irish monastery consisted of a cluster of dwelling huts grouped round one church building or more which might be of wood or stone, and a scriptorium. The churches were usually, though not always, rather small. Ideally, this "City of God" was enclosed by a circle of crosses though, no doubt because of the expense, this seems to have remained rather an ideal to be aimed at.

The brethren of these monasteries might well find themselves called to carry the Gospel to other lands and the period of Irish missionary activity was one of the greatest in the history of Christianity. It is also the worst documented. Both Roman and English interests have combined in self-interest to suppress this chapter in the history of Europe.

Columban missionaries from Iona founded the abbey on Lindisfarne, in the territory seized by the Angles: the first meaningful attempt to bring civilisation to the pagan Teutons—and its success was incredible. Within a few years a steady stream of scholars was leaving England for higher education in Irish schools; students' grants being available for necessitous cases. To take but one example, a certain Cynefrid was appointed Abbot in the young Abbey of Jarrow, but, after a year or two, he resigned (circa 660) in order to go to Ireland to improve his education, and he was one of many.

In the meantime, Irish missionaries had been busy in many other directions. About 590 Columbanus of Bangor went to the Continent. He settled first in a derelict Roman fort at Annegray in the Vosges. From there he moved to Luxeuil but fell foul of Theuderic of Burgundy. He moved on to Jouarre and in due course he and his disciples founded houses at Faremoutiers, Rebans, St. Gall in Switzerland and Bobbio, south of Milan. Another interesting character was Willibrord, an Englishman trained in Ireland. He was sent off to convert Frisia to the Faith. He did so, going on from there to found the Bishopric of Utrecht and a monastery at Echternach in Luxembourg.

A certain Kilian converted Franconia and Thuringia. He was murdered at Wurzburg in 698. Other Irish foundations were at Fursa, Peronne, Lagny, near Paris and Honau on the Rhine.

This gives some idea of the extent of the work carried out by these too often forgotten saints, during the 6th and 7th centuries.

Significantly, Aldhelm of Malmsbury, circa 685, talks of "boatloads" of Englishmen going to Ireland to study grammar, geometry, physics and so on and he points out how unnecessary and even undesirable this is when there are plenty of excellent teachers at home in England. In other words, Europe was beginning to recover from the disaster of 410 and, in spite of the terror which the word "Mahommed" evoked, civilisation was once more established firmly and Ireland's period of usefulness was drawing to a close. Ireland might have remained a force to be reckoned with had it not been for a rather unfortunate and stupid quarrel.

To lesser mortals it might not seem very important if Easter were to be celebrated on one weekend rather than another, but theologians are not lesser mortals. By the first half of the seventh century, the Columban Order had become rich, powerful and rather aggressive and a bitter quarrel now broke out between Iona and Rome over the correct method of computing Easter. Iona's daughter house of Lindisfarne in Northumbria found itself in the very heart of the fight because Rome had recently established a mission station at Canterbury in the south, and was most anxious to expand. The two sides came together for a serious discussion at the village of Whitby, where St. Wilfred put the case for Rome well and clearly, pointing out that Rome was much more powerful than Ireland and therefore Rome must obviously be correct! For better or for worse, the Northumbrian king came down in favour of Rome with the inevitable result that the centre of power, first ecclesiastical and then temporal, moved south leaving Northumbria the depressed backwater it has remained to this day and, most significantly for the future, breaking the long-established ties of friendship between the North of England and the Dal Riada which was soon to become Scotland.

One other feature of the Irish Church should be noted. As the Church grew it became both wealthy and worldly. Wealth and ostentation, quarrelling and feuding are not acceptable within the Christian fold and, as so often happens, a young and idealistic generation appeared, determined to put things right. So was born the movement of the Culdees, the Vassals of God. The movement appears to have originated in the South, in a rather insignificant monastery at Dairinnis —then an islet in the Blackwater estuary, now joined to the mainland. The corner-stone of the movement was the three-fold demand: asceticism/puritanism/ stricter monasticism. Many attempts have been made to present the Céile-Dé, or Culdee movement as a forward-looking evangelical movement and even to see in it a first, hesitant step towards the Reformation of the 16th century. It is obviously both easy and tempting to overstate the case.

To return. The Culdee movement proved an instant success and spread like wildfire throughout Ireland. Armagh, Clonmacnois, Glendalough and a host of smaller houses declared for the Culdees. Next we find them in Scotland where they proved even more popular than in Ireland.[1] They survived, in some measure at least, the compulsory reforms of Queen Margaret's time and seem to have maintained their principles long after the Irish Church had become a matter of history. Eventually, the last remnants of them appear to have been absorbed into the Augustinians, the Canons Regular or Teaching Friars.[2]

However, we are again running ahead. Much was to happen before Culdees became Augustinians. Ireland, as we saw, had escaped two periods of horror and bloodshed: she did not escape the third. During the year 793 strange ships appeared off the Northumbrian coast. They came to land at Lindisfarne where their crews set to work to chase away and kill the monks and to fill their pockets with the wealth of the Abbey. The Viking Age had dawned. From the fire-seared ruins the surviving monks carried to safety the body of the saintly Cuthbert who had piloted the monastery through the unhappy period after Whitby, with a few more of their treasures but most of these priceless objects went back to Norway with the raiders. This pattern was to be repeated with sickening regularity year after year. We shall deal with the doings of the Norse in a later chapter so here a brief summary will suffice.

In 795 Iona's turn came and it was burned thereafter with such regularity that in 825, after the Abbot Blathmac had been killed in the course of the looting, Iona was abandoned and nearly three hundred years of dedicated labour in the service of God and humanity was brought to a close. What might Iona have given the world had it not been for these cruel years? The so-called Book of Kells, more properly the Book of Iona, gives us a hint of what the Columban Order had to offer the world. It was not to be. The Order had been under continual fire from Rome since the time of the Easter controversy. In 717 Nechtan, the Pictish king, following the lead of Northumbria and encouraged by a Canterbury which had itself a very poor record in the field of conversion to the Christian Faith, expelled the Columban clergy from his territories. Although this cruel decision was later rescinded, ruined Iona could no longer claim to be the centre of the Scottish Church and the religious centre of a land shortly to become Scotland moved to Dunkeld.

From 836 on things slowly improved. Faced with the choice between Christ and Thor, people had to choose the more attractive figure and when in the year 1000 the Icelandic Thing[3] met to decide which was to be the religion of the country, Thor didn't stand a chance. Here was the culmination of two hundred years of patient teaching, partly, at least, by the Irish. As the final decision was to be taken, a great storm of thunder and rain broke over the meeting and the older generation declared that the old gods were angry, but it was too late; the Powers of Asgard were vanquished. "Yol" became the birthday of Jesus, the "blot" was replaced by the bread and wine of the Eucharist and, although pagan practices did linger on, the number of those who understood their significance grew smaller and smaller until by about 1150 even the great Temple of Uppsala in Sweden was in ruins.[4]

In Ireland itself, the Norse power was completely broken in 1014 when Brian Boraimhe defeated the Norse at Clontarf. The Church, however, had to take a fresh look at itself, as Canterbury was now showing a most improper interest in the affairs of Ireland, even to the extent of appointing a bishop to the Diocese of Dublin, using as excuse the fact that the Irish Church had no metropolitan bishop of its own. Times had changed; it was proper now for the old abbots to bow out with a good grace and to make way for complete unity with Rome.

Scotland followed much the same course. Iona was restored after 900 but its glory had departed. As a rather small and mean Benedictine monastery it survived until the Reformation and even after, but the need for such a centre was now gone and from the 17th until the 19th century the abbey church served as a cowshed! The Irishisms of the Scottish Church were evidently ironed out by Queen Margaret and by, say 1100 the old ways were no more than a memory, the Irish type monasteries being now all replaced by the Continental orders.

After this brief review, we can return to deal with Columba and other saints of his time. As will be seen, the history of the Irish Church, as indeed the history of Ireland itself, is a story of half-realised possibilities and wasted potentialities.

Of the dozens of Irish saints who laboured diligently and faithfully, one name stands out as pre-eminent among them—Columba, and as we have a reasonably full and accurate account of his life and work, we may well take him as typical.

47

Columba was born about 521 or 522. Here is his family tree:—

Niall nan Naoi Giall, Ard-rígh Eireann
|
Conall Gulban
|
Fergus
|
Fedilmith = Eithne
|
Crimthann (Columba).

As will be seen, his parentage was illustrious but this did not deter him from the life of hardship he had chosen.

His original name was Crimthann, said to mean "fox", and Columba, the Dove, was a name chosen when he entered the monastic life. In Gaelic he is always Calum-Cille, the Dove of the Church.

As a boy, Columba was trained by a priest called Cruithnechan. He is said also to have studied under Bishop Findbarr but there is some doubt as to who this man was. He apparently also had a master called Gemman.

Tradition says his first foundation was Derry. He was certainly implicated in a battle at a place called Cul-drebene, near Sligo, between the northern and the southern branches of the O'Neill family and it may just possibly be the case that it was a sense of guilt after that battle that made him decide to dedicate his life to work in distant lands—(It is known that he was for a time excommunicated from the Church). It is certain that he left for Scotland about two years later, in or about 563, and that he was back in Ireland about 575 attending a council held at Druimm-cete where various far-reaching decisions appear to have been taken including one to grant autonomy to Scottish Dal Riada—the future Scotland. About ten years later he was back in Ireland when he founded a new abbey at Dairmag (Oak-tree Plain—Durrow in Co. Offaly).

In the meantime he travelled extensively throughout Scotland, making friends with the local people. He founded a number of monasteries which have disappeared so completely that, at present at least, we can do little more than guess at the situation. They include Hinba (probably Colonsay), Cailli aufinde (somewhere on the mainland), Maglunge in Tiree, Cella Diuni on Loch Aweside and, probably, Elena. He visited Islay, Mull, Skye, Ardnamurchan, Rannoch, The Great Glen, Inverness and so on.

His favourite monastery was Iona and there he died on the evening of 8th June, 597. His death being marked by many supernatural portents (as was the custom of the time!).

The picture we get of life in a Columban monastery is a rather attractive one. We see Columba as an efficient administrator, skilled in politics and worldly affairs as well as an educationist and "father". We see him not afraid to speak his mind when necessary (122a), but genuinely concerned with the welfare of the brethren (31b, 77b). An approachable man (87b), one need never be afraid to confess shortcomings to him and seek his help. The monastery has a relaxed, happy atmosphere with none of the grim, unlovely, puritanical asceticism of, say, a Cistercian house.

We read of the monks working in the fields, gathering winter food, watched by the elderly Columba (38a), of the clumsy oaf upsetting the ink (29a). Of the thief forgiven and fed (42ab), of the monks tending a sick bird (47b et seq.) and so on. Perhaps the pleasantest tale is that of the old white horse mourning for its master (127ab). (The figures refer to the pages as given in the Andersons' text of the life of Columba).[5]

The route he followed between Ireland and Scotland seems more than difficult to re-discover. A poem speaks of Columba sailing from Lough Foyle and while the poem is admittedly late, it seems most likely that it was from his home territory that he set out. Tradition tells us that he landed first in Kintyre, but it is a little hard to see why he should sail through the dangerous water off the north and north-east of Ireland, parallel to the shore, when the mouth of Lochindaal lay invitingly before him, a relatively easy sail.

While that was almost certainly the first stage of his voyage, we have no way of telling which side of Islay he sailed up then, though there is perhaps a slight bias in favour of the east coast. At any rate, Texa is almost certainly the isle of Oidech on which Cainneach, who forgot his crozier, landed, showing that he, at least used the east route. Further, there is a dedication to Columba at the mouth of the Laggan which may mark his resting-place and there is a similar site near Ardbeg on the East, with a tradition of his having landed here. Again, if Ardnave does contain "nemeton", it is a fair guess that it was still a pagan sanctuary and prudence would suggest that it be given a wide berth.

Islay does not figure prominently in the biography,[5] not unreasonably so if it had only recently been subdued but we do read of a dishonest Islayman who murdered a Pict entrusted to his care by Columba and who died in the same autumn before he could taste pigs' flesh fattened on the fruit of trees. Tradition says that this gentleman lived at Eilean na Muice Duibh (Island Farm = Isle of the Black Pig) and as this lies beside the Columban site at Laggan, perhaps this may be right. The "fruit of trees" eaten by pigs is normally acorns, and Eigedale (Oakdale) is reasonably close nearby (cf. 71 ab).

What is true for Columba is, we may assume, more or less the same for the lesser names. Columba's nearest important rival was Clonmacnois, founded by Ciaran on an esker on the Shannon (Co. Offaly). Ciaran (older Ceran) was slightly older than Columba. One church in Islay bears his name, and indeed, may originally have been an oratory of the older Irish type. Earnan was the uncle of Columba and sailed with him to Scotland. He may be the saint commemorated in Killernadal (Jura) = (Church of) Ernan's dale (Norse).

Once settled, after the invasions of the sons of Erc, Islay must have become a centre for anchorites and for religious studies, though there is, alas, no written evidence to support this. We depend on the very large number of church names for this conclusion.

The fact that so many saints chose Islay as a specially holy place reminds us of the long period of peace in the Isles from the time of the settlement of the sons of Erc until the coming of the Norse. Years during which almost all the rest of civilised Europe knew nothing but the horror of wars and invasions.

Parish Names

Parish boundaries are not lines drawn on a map by a civil servant or Government flunkey. They grew up over hundreds of years, first as the divisions between the territories of petty rulers in tribal times and thus they continue with probably few alterations down to the present day. It is a little hard to see why one church rather than another should become the chief place of worship and give its name to the parish but it does no more than reflect the needs of an early time when the most convenient building would normally be chosen as the centre. This does not hold good for Kildalton where the church chosen was in the least convenient part of the parish. Here sentiment probably entered in.

The present parishes are:—

Kilarrow: Maol Rubha's Church. Maol Rubha was a monk of Bangor, near Belfast. He died in 722.

Kilchiaran: Ciaran's Church. Probably, though not certainly, this is Ciaran, Abbot of Clonmacnois, County Offaly, an older contemporary of Columba.

Kilchoman: Coman's Church. This is probably the nephew of Fergno, 4th Abbot of Iona. Floruit circa 640.

Kildalton: The Fosterling's Church.

Kilmeny: A doubtful dedication. Possibly this is Eithne, mother of Columba.

Fuller notes on these are given in the Appendix.

There are chapels in various other places the names of which have been lost. In Texa there is a chapel dedicated to the Virgin, on, apparently, the scene of the miraculous recovery of Cainneach's crozier. At the foot of Gleann A' Ghaoith there is what appears to have been a fairly important religious settlement. This may have been the scene of Norse atrocities as even the name has been lost and folklore has only vague unsatisfactory accounts of the site.

Baile an Aba (Balinaby)—the Abbot's Township (Kilchoman) and Lòn an t-Sagairt—the Priest's field at Kildalton are memorials of the lands set aside to maintain the church. The former, at least of these names, is pre-Norse as the Aba has a long initial vowel, unlike the modern word.

With the gradual substitution of Roman ways for the old Scottish church came also a change of vocabulary. The word "Cille" dropped out of use and a new borrowing took its place—eaglais, from the Greek.

Another interesting change came in personal names. During these early years of Christianity, it was fashionable for a holy man to have the hair tonsured. Roman churchmen shaved the crown of the head and Columban churchmen shaved from the forehead back (this reflects the pattern of balding—Celts tend to bald from the forehead and Latins more commonly show baldness first on the crown). The tonsure, and its wearer were called "maol", hence we have such names as Miles—Maol Iosa—the tonsured servant of Jesus, and Malcolm—Maol Chaluim = the Tonsured Servant of Columba. From the end of the tenth century a new fashion in names appears. Maol vanishes and another word, gille = a servant lad, takes its place: Gilles = Gille Iosa, the Servant of Jesus; Gilchrist = Gille Chriosd = the Servant of Christ; Gilmour = Gille Moire = the Servant of Mary. Notice too that Biblical names are now beginning to replace the old Irish habit of giving dedications to local saints, just as the change from maol to gille probably reflects the change to the Roman tonsure.

[1] As late as the 11th century we find Malcolm III (1070–1093) making a grant of land to the Keledei of Lochleven.

[2] Edward Dwelly in his Gaelic Dictionary translates Culdee, inter alia, as Keeper of the Fire. Where he got this gem of information I have not the remotest idea. If it is correct, it opens a huge field for speculation: were these Culdees, in any sense, a revival of the old druidic priest hood? On the face of it, it seems improbable but the religious centre at Kildare was certainly a "fire" sanctuary in pagan times and there were others of the same sort. It is highly probable that there was some sort of vague relationship between the fire sanctuaries of Western Europe and the older religions of Greece and Persia.

[3] Parliament.

Uppsala means Upper Room, i.e. place near to the home of the gods, cf. the "High Places" mentioned in the Old Testament and the story of the Tower of Babel, the "Upper Room" of Babylon (Genesis Ch. 11).

[5] Adomnan: Life of St. Columba, ed. Anderson, A. O. and M. O. (Nelson).

APPENDIX

In addition to these churches named, there is an astonishing number of lesser cells. There are not as many as in the Isle of Man, but there are quite enough to make it obvious that the island was a centre of religious activity, the very nature of which is now forgotten so one can only assume that it was part of a movement unpopular with the "official" Christian Church of Western Europe. Possibly further research into the Culdee movement and its offshoots may throw light on this.

The following is a list, almost certainly incomplete, of the early churches. The list was compiled by Mr. Gilbert Clark, Port Charlotte but the comments on it are mine and I accept responsibility for errors. Here I must point out that there can often be great difficulty in locating a site. I have myself, on more than one occasion spent hours searching for an alleged site without success and in one or two of the examples which follow I cannot claim to have found the site but I have reasonable grounds for supposing that it does actually exist.

Kilinallan (various spellings) Cille an Àilein—This name occurs twice to my knowledge: at Loch Gruineirt and at Kildalton. Local tradition associates it with a St. Allan, otherwise unknown but, as it stands, it means Church on the Greensward.

Kilarrow—Cille Mhaoil Rubha. Maol Rubha is the saint of Loch Maree. The original settlement was at Bridgend, near the Drochaid Tioram but Campbell of Islay had the new village of Bowmore built with its Round Church and the old village and church were demolished. He came from Ireland to Applecross in 671 and died in 722. He is often called, wrongly, an abbot of Bangor.

Cill Bhrannain—Brendan's Church—near Mulindry.

Kilbride—Cille Bhride (St. Brigit) (?) of Kildare's Church (Port Ellen).

Cill Chaluim Chille-Callumkill, Ardbeg; Keills, Port Askaig; Nerabus; (?) Lossit, Kilmeny; (?) Orsay (and probably another site at Laggan). All these being dedications to St Columba founded, we may assume, by his followers.

Cill Chatain—Cattan's Church, Oa. Gille Chatain (Cattan's Lad) is the eponymous ancestor of the Macintoshes and their related families.

Kilcavan, Kealsa, Rhinns. Said to commemorate St. Kevan of Glendalough. I have no further information regarding this site.

Cille mo Cheallaig—There are two sites bearing the name: Laggan and Oa. Probably the saint is Ceallach, Abbot of Iona 802–815, i.e. during the worst period of Norse raiding and just before the Columban Order abandoned Iona.

Kilchenzie—Cille Chainnich, Mackenzie Island. If this Cainnech is Cainnech of Aghadh Bó, the absent-minded friend of Columba, and if this is indeed the island on which he found his staff, then all theories on the early divisions of Islay must fall.

Kilichiaran—Cille Chiarain. There were several saints called Ciaran, but the famous one was Ciaran of Clonmacnois (Cluan mac Nois), Co. Offaly, who died about 549 and who, in Ireland ranks with Columba. The old name for Campbeltown is Ceann Loch Cille Chiarain (Loch Kilkerran Head) and it is still Ceann Locha in Gaelic.

Kilchoman—Cille Chomain, Rhinns. Probably the Coman mentioned by Adomnan as the nephew of Fergno, fourth Abbot of Iona.

Cill Chomhgain, Oa.—Perhaps the man called Comgan Céle Dé who appears to have belonged to Co. Roscommon. There was another of the name who came from Leinster and who died circa 730.

Cille Chuibein, Kildalton—Said to be a dedication to Kevan of Glendalough but I cannot see the connection. I believe it to be a dedication to a saint otherwise unknown.

Kildalton—Cill Daltan. This is said to be a dedication to John the Beloved, Fosterling of God. It is strange that this fact was not known to the minister of Kildalton in the middle of last century (cf. New Stat. Acc. Kildalton Parish).

Cill Eathain, Oa—This is the name which gives Iain in Scotland, Sean in Ireland and John in English. It is originally Hebrew: "God is Gracious". Dedication to Biblical saints were rare in the old Irish Church but I am told that this same dedication occurs in Strath Brora.

Cill Eileagan, Kilmeny and (?) Gruineart. I know nothing about this saint.

Kilellan—The saint is Faelan or Faolan (the Wolf), but as there were at least sixteen saints of the name, we cannot tell which is intended. This name occurs at St. Fillan's and Bruce, the night before Bannockburn, is said to have placed himself under the protection of St. Fillan, styled Faolan amlabhar—the dumb, a descendent of Core of Cashel in Munster (Watson, Place-names, p. 285).

Kilennan—Cill Fhionain. This Fionan was styled Lobar—diseased, infirm, and was a native of Munster. His name is found at Kilfinnan and other places.

Cill Lasrach, Port Ellen—This commemorates a female saint called Lasair and three of the names are known but the name, which means "flame" may have another and deeper significance here (cf. p. 27).

Cill Luchaig, Laphroaig—This St. Luchag (Little Mouse) was a female. As far as I know, the only other occurence of her name in Scotland is Clach mo Luchaig, near Fortingall, a stone to which scolds were once fastened.

Kilmeny—Cille Mheanaidh. It has been suggested that this name commemorates Eithne, mother of Columba, but the phonetics are doubtful. The name may be the same as in Dalmeny, West Lothian and it is perhaps more probable that it commemorates a saint otherwise unknown. Local explanations include Cille a' Mhanaich—the Monk's Church and Cille a' Mheadhoin—the Church of the Middle (section of the island). These are both highly improbable.

Cill Muire—St. Mary's Church. There are two sites bearing the name: Lagavullin and Texa. These are dedications to the Virgin. This dedication is found again at Kilmory, Knapdale, but I am told that Kilmore, near Oban, is just the Big Church.

Kilnave—Cill Néimh. There are four known saints of the name.

Kilnaughton—Cill Neachdain (the initial N- is not sounded in the Cille though it is sounded in Baile Neachdain). There were at least two saints of the name; one from Eastern Scotland and the other from Co. Derry. The name occurs as Mo-Neachdan in Iona.

Cill Ronain, near Loch Corr—Probably this is Ronan, Abbot of Kingarth in Bute who died about 737. He has a church on the now deserted island of North Rona (Norse: St. Ronan's Isle), but, as Watson correctly points out (Place-names, p. 309), this is not the saint of Rona, near Skye, which is simply Norse: Rough Isle—cf. Robolls—Rough Steading.

Cill Sléibhin, Port Askaig—Sleibhine, was one of Columba's successors in Iona. He died about 767.

Cill Thomhain, Oa—I have no information about this site or its saint.

Eaglais Iolarain—(Conisby) is said to be a dedication to St. Hilary, who was one of the Fathers of the Early Church.

Finlaggan—Insula S. Finlagani in Yle is mentioned in 1427 and the remains of the chapel still stand to a fair height though a good deal of the building, including the east wall has fallen in recent years. The present structure dates from about 1350–60 and was erected by the Good John of Islay. Watson tells us (Place-names p. 304) that Finlaggan is a diminutive of Findlug. The name appears as a surname in the Oa during the 17th century.

An odd name is Cille Bholg, near Gartmain. This appears to mean Church of the Bellies. This is certainly the local understanding of the name but one is tempted to wonder if it might just possibly contain the ancient Bolg, found in Fir Bolg, Belgium, etc. and meaning "shining" or the like.

There is a chapel on Eilean Néimh for which no separate name seems to have survived. Other nameless chapels are found at Ardmore (a probable site), Glen a' Gaoith, Rhinns and, I am told, Tallant, Toradale and Ardlarach, though I personally have not found them. At least in the case of the Glen a' Gaoith chapel, the loss of the name is almost certainly due to Norse destruction of the site during the Viking Period.

Burial grounds, now nameless, are found in several other places and these too must originally have been under the protection of some saint.

The island on Loch Lossit is said by Dean Monroe to have belonged to the Bishop of the Isles in his time i.e. just before the Reformation, but he does not say what sort of building stood on it. The island is wooded and, although foundations can be seen, it is hard to make out any coherent plan.

The most noteworthy pagan sites have been mentioned in the text but excavation should reveal interesting foundations at Cladh Dubhain and at Cladh Haco (which may be pagan Norse). Another site which must be excavated before any useful comment can be made on it lies under the eastern slope of Beinn Tart a' Mhill.

CHAPTER 6

THE ISLAND NAMES

Our best collection of Early Scottish place-names comes from a source sufficiently interesting to merit some mention.

As we have seen, the collapse of the Roman Empire led, not to the joyous heavenly bliss foretold by the writer of the Book of the Revelation (cf. Rev. 17–19) but to misery and chaos throughout the whole known world. Yet all through these terrible years civilisation did, somehow, manage to stay alive. During the very worst period Ireland remained as the home of European scholarship but, even then, there were those on the Continent who dreamed of rebuilding the ancient ruins. The political administration of the Empire was gone for ever but, underlying even that, was a basic framework of sympathetic feeling, sustained largely by the young and vigorous Christian Church, centred on Rome. While it is, of course, impossible to summarise in a few lines the outlook of any one period in history, nevertheless one may say that, by the seventh century, there was a general feeling that the worst was over and that now, by the help of men of good-will, stability and imperialism (more or less synonymous terms) could be restored. What, then, more natural than that men should see the Church not only as a spiritual but also as a secular leader! Indeed, at this stage the Church showed itself well worthy of men's trust. Prudently and wisely (allowing, of course, for the odd human error), the Church manipulated its allies slowly but surely to rebuild the fabric of the old Empire and when, in 800 A.D., the Pope himself crowned in solemn state an "Emperor" for this new "Holy Roman Empire"—really a loose confederacy of more-or-less friendly states—it seemed that men might say, "Finis coronat opus". This, at any rate, was the feeling of the Church and, having attended to the West, it was felt that things there could now be left ticking over quietly, as the time had come to deal with the East.

Again, by skilful handling, much was accomplished. Soon most of the Holy Land had been recovered from the Muslims and in 1014, Godfrey de Bouillon entered the Holy City itself in triumph, delighting everyone by refusing to don a crown of gold in the place where his Saviour had worn a crown of thorns.

Unfortunately, the seeds of decay and dissolution were inherent in the Church's very success. A dictatorship can flourish only for as long as those subject to it are prepared to accept its authority and, while Western Europe by and large was prepared to accept the supremacy of the Papacy, Eastern Europe and the Middle East most decidedly were not. So it came about that, after the conquest of the Holy Places by the soldiers of the new Roman Empire, Christians, native to Palestine who had lived peacefully for generations under Muslim rule— tolerated, if hardly encouraged—now found themselves subjected to hostile criticism and, indeed, active persecution by brother Christians who insisted, on what authority it is hard to say, that the Papal writ ran throughout Christendom. The end was in sight when the hostilities against the infidel were suspended indefinitely in favour of a spirited and bloody attack on the Eastern Church.

This foolish arrogance brought its own reward. The Holy Land Kingdom of Outremer, the whole of Asia Minor and even the great Christian city of Constantinople were lost for ever. Islam had triumphed!

After this ghastly fiasco, Western Europe too came to question more and more insistently the genuineness of the Papal claims, and, indeed, the wisdom of the whole "imperial" system. The enthusiasm for empire building was gone and, to cut a long story short, the final collapse of the old Eastern Empire before Islam provided the impetus for open revolt against the Papacy in the West. The last remnants of the corpse of the Holy Roman Empire were more or less decently interred by Napoleon and the broken and fragmented Western Christian Church was left to lick its wounds.

All this disaster, however, lay far in the future at the time with which we are dealing: a time when young folk all over Europe were dreaming of a better world and groups of enthusiasts were busily trying to turn dreams into reality. At this time the North of Italy, rather than Rome itself which still lay largely in ruins, was the centre of Europe and in Ravenna round about 670 A.D., a monk, whose name unfortunately has been forgotten, fired with the spirit of the times, set himself the task of re-drawing on paper the bounds of the Empire and preparing a list of the ancient Imperial possessions.

He had, apparently found a bundle of old Roman Army itineraries and, armed with these, he now painstakingly prepared a sort of "Gazeteer of our Empire". He had quite a lot of material on Britain but, of course, all of it was out of date; there is absolutely no trace of any post-Roman influence on his British names. In other words, his names reflect, not the Britain of the seventh century, but the Britain of some 300–400 years earlier.

Although all his names are interesting and repay study, we here are most concerned with his lists of island names which appear to have been taken from the log of a naval commander on a reconnaissance expedition. He gives us a list of fourteen or fifteen names of Scottish islands. He then goes on to say, "in another place are said to lie . . ." and he gives a list of a further twelve Scottish island names. Again, in another chapter, he lists another four British islands, two of which certainly belong to the South but the other two, Malaca and Insenos, may be Irish or Northern—the latter looks as if it contained the Old Irish inis = an island.

Here we have to realise that many island names have changed over the centuries. Whole communities had their customs, character and even languages changed by the coming of Christian missionaries and Norse settlers—gently by the missionaries, rather more roughly by the Norse! What, for example, was the name of Inchmarnock before the saintly Earnan settled there? It now means

55

St. Earnan's isle. Or again what did the natives call Pabbay—Priest Isle before the Norse pagans bestowed that title on it? As we shall see, we have several sources of information, but our friend from Ravenna supplies by far the largest number of names. The other two main sources are:—Adomnan the biographer of St. Columba. He was the ninth Abbot of Iona and died on 23rd Sept., 704 (as Columba, himself, the first Abbot, died just over a hundred years earlier, it would seem that abbots of Iona were not noted for longevity!) and, second, Ptolemy of Alexandria who wrote a treatise on the theory of geography around about 130–140 A.D. Like Ravenna he appears to be a little out of date for he makes no mention of Hadrian's Wall which was some 15–20 years old when he wrote. And, indeed, although he is slightly out of date for Britain, he is demonstrably hundreds of years out of date for Ireland for which, of course, no Roman records were available as no major landings were ever made in Ireland.

Other names crop up incidentally in the Irish Annals but one may mention the deplorable destruction of the historical records of the Highlands and Islands. So successful have been the attempts to "extirpate the Highlanders, root and branch" that, from some four hundred years of Norse rule, not one single document, not one single written word survives which was demonstrably written in the Western Isles and from the entire life-time of the Lordship of the Isles we have but one solitary (and virtually illegible) Gaelic title-deed (it is dated 6th May 1408 from, apparantly, Finlaggan and is signed by Donald, second Lord). It is for this reason that we treasure so highly the Latin writings of a foreign monk who never in his life saw Scotland and knew not one word of Gaelic.

Here are the names given by the Ravenna monk and, in spite of his saying "in another place", the two lists appear to run parallel. Possibly List A consists of places visited by the fleet and List B of islands seen and named by the pilot:—

LIST A	LIST B
Corsula	Magnancia
Mona	Anas
Regaina	Atina
Minerve	Elete
Cunis	Daroeda
Manna	Esse
Botis	Gra (n)dena
Vinion	Maiona
Saponis	Longis
Susura	Erimon/Eirimon
Birila	Exosades, where precious stones grow.
Elviana	
Sobrica	
Scetis	
Linnonsa	

In addition we have, from Chapter V:—

Malaca

Insenos.

56

Several familiar names will be noticed at once, but obviously the work is less valuable than it might have been had the spelling been better. Probably the original log-book entries were none too accurate (Romans, like English, made a point of not being able to understand or pronounce foreign words) and generations of copyists have all contributed their quotas of errors. Sometimes we can correct the names either from Adomnan or from the modern forms; in other places we can but guess at what is intended. One of the worthy monk's more disconcerting habits is his trick of sticking on apparently random beginnings and endings so that one cannot be quite sure what is name and what is mere "padding".

The first name of List A appears to be merely the departure point—Corsula, which we still have in Norse dress in Corsewall Point. The fleet then proceeds to Mona = Isle of Man[1] and thence to Regaina = Rathlin. We then enter the Firth of Clyde where we have Minerve, Cunis, Manna, Botis. Botis and Manna must be Bute and Arran (Gaelic Bod = (?) Fire place and Arainn = Place of the (god) Aru), but the other two are more difficult. Cunis suggests Cone and so Ailsa Craig—but why bother visiting Ailsa Craig? Minerve is generally regarded as a translation into Latin = Place of Minerva, but perhaps, as in Manna, we should ignore the M-. This leaves Iner(v) which could be Inis . . . and probably = Inchmarnock or Holy Isle off Lamlash.

At this point the expedition leaves the Clyde, returning to Vinion [which occurs elsewhere as Avoyn (meaning unknown) and now bears the Norse name Sanda = Sand isle—off Kintyre], and heads north. Now, if we assume the names to be more or less in order (and all theories fall if they are not), we find the fleet moving through the Sound of Jura, avoiding Islay and Gigha, but stopping at Sa(p)onis[2] which is the island Saine(a) mentioned by Adomnan and which, as we will see later, is Jura. At the north end of Jura the ships bear W.N.W., call at Susura and proceed to Birila = beyond reasonable doubt, Tiree (Tir Idhe). Susura is quite impossible. It cannot be Iona = I, or Colonsay = Hinb (as we shall see). Just possibly Scarba is not a Norse name but a Norse rendering of this S(usu)r(a).

After Birila, Elviana is visited. Now this was an island well-known and important in antiquity. It is given its correct form, Elen(a) by Adomnan and he mentions that a certain Lugbe was prior of a monastery there. Further, the name occurs in the Annals of Ulster—Daoiread Eilein—the enslavement of Elen. If the name had survived and been allowed to develop naturally, it would have become Eilean—almost exactly the same sound as the modern Gaelic eilean = island, but quite unrelated for eilean is just a borrowing from Norse, ey land[3]. It is interesting, however, to note that this name occurs elsewhere in Scotland. On the Clyde Estuary we have Inellan = An Eilean in Gaelic and much time and ingenuity have been devoted to explaining away this non-existent island. Had it really been "Island" we would, of course, have An t-Eilean as eilean is masculine.

Elen, with Sobrica, lies between Tiree and Scetis = Skye and it is very tempting to see it in *Eilean* nam Muc = Muck, but that island appears never to have had a monastery. Rum and Eigg also appear to be impossible, as we shall

57

see, and we are left with two possibilities: Canna or the Uists. The latter is tempting for, in spite of its Norse dress, Canna may well be an ancient name while Uist is certainly Norse. Again North Uist has distinct traces of an early Columban site—like Iona it has a nearby Port nan Long (Ship Bay), Port nan Curragh in Iona, and also an adjacent Oransay = Oran's isle just as Colonsay has.

On the other hand, the general impression we have is of a fleet sailing a fairly direct course towards Skye and not zig-zagging from isle to isle and when one finds that Canna also boasts an early Columban site, this tempts me at least into giving it the casting vote. My guess is that Elviana = mod. Canna, though what Canna itself may mean I have no idea.

The next island, Sobrica would appear to parallel the Engaricena mentioned by Ptolemy but its location is a puzzle, especially as Ptolemy may be referring to Rathlin—which this obviously cannot be. The obvious island is Eigg but here we have no similarity to the early forms of the name from Irish sources. The Irish Annals mention the murder of St. Donnan on the 17th April of the year 618. Here the name of the island appears as Ego, Aego, Ega, associated in one case with a word "dine" of unknown meaning. There is no trace of any "ric".

The next port of call is beyond dispute. Scetis = Skye, An t-Eilean Sgitheanach and this is followed by one more name, Linnonsa, which is probably a corrupt form of the name which the Norse were to turn into Leoðus = Lewis (The letters n and v are easily confused and this name may originally have stood as Livvous or the like).

Having completed the course of the voyage, we may now turn to List B, probably either places seen but not visited, or visited on another journey, so we start again in the Firth of Clyde and round Kintyre as before.

This list starts with Magnancia and Annas—presumably Great Annas and Annas and the two Cumbraes lie ready to hand. Their present names date from the early Christian period. As for the meaning, cf. Anu, the Irish Mother of the Gods. The correct form would then probably be Anainn = Place of Anu.

Next we have Cana, Atina and Elete. Atina must be the name which occurs in Adomnan as Aithche and in a survey of Dalriada as Oideach, long ago identified with Texa and, of course, Ele(te) is Ile = Islay. Cana, then, must be Gigha (Norse Guð ey). Probably this is for Cara for this is still the name of an islet off Gigha usually explained as Copse isle (Norse) but as it is treeless, this seems unconvincing. The meaning is doubtful but we may compare Carrodunon = Krappitz on the Oder. It cannot be the British word Caer = a fort.

The next recognisable name is Maiona which is, beyond reasonable doubt, for Malios = Muile—Mull, a word meaning something like "pre-eminent". Daroeda, Esse and Gra(n)dena must then lie between Jura and Mull. If we assume that the fleet continued north past Texa and Islay and the East of Jura, then the Corrievreckan currents would deter any commander not personally acquainted with the waters from seeking an outlet westwards through them. He would be far more likely to proceed north past Scarba and through the opening between Lunga and Luing. Now Luing lies close against the mainland and is most inconspicuous; the next name we can expect is the name the pilot gave for Lunga (now Norse, Heather isle) and this I take to be Daroeda, whatever that may mean.

Next they would see the Garvellochs, Mull, and then Iona. Iona is I, Ia or Ie and this suggests E(ss)e but, if this is correct, then Gra(n)dena (= ? Cliff Place) is out of order for this is surely the island that St. Brendan called Aileach (Cliff Place) and which is recorded on the O.S. map (wrongly), as Eileach an Naoimh (for Na h-Eileacha Naomha—the Garvellochs). The only other possibility would be Staffa and, as it is really uninhabitable, this seems less likely.

Longos and Erimon we can take together. Remove the first letter of the latter and we have Rimon. This name is the older form of Rum. It appears elsewhere as Ruimean, Rúmind and Ruimind (Irish Annals) where, under 677 we have recorded the death of St. Beccan of Rum while Dean Donald Monro, who visited the island circa 1549, says that the older folk called it Ronin. The meaning is unknown and the word is almost certainly pre-Indo-European.

Longos is harder. It can have no connection with the mod. Gaelic word long = a ship which was a later borrowing from Latin, longa navis. Ptolemy mentions a river called Long by which he appears to mean the modern Loch Long (mod. Loch nan Long = Loch of the Ships possibly by popular etymology), while Adomnan has an island "which in Latin may be called Long" and by this he probably means the Long Island and, indeed this may well be the meaning here. On the other hand—and this is no more than a very tentative suggestion— if we treat this word as we did Erimon and remove the first letter, we are left with Ong (is) and further, if we remember that the writer has earlier confused n and r, we get Org for which we can read Orc for orc is, in Old Celtic, a pig. It is, in fact, the name we get in Orkney which means originally Pig-tribe place. Now it is most unlikely that Orkney is intended here but just next door to Rum is Muck, Eilean nam Muc = Pig Isle just exactly where it ought to be if the list is in order. The -is may well be the correct ending for this could make it mean something like Pig-tribe Place.

One name remains, Exosades, and Lethbridge (The Painted Men) rather cleverly identified this with the Shiant Isles, pointing out that the felspar caves are obviously the precious stone place. These isles certainly lie more or less where, according to the list, it ought to be and the word does indeed look like a plural, though it is, no doubt, corrupt like the others. Again if we assume that the Ex- is just Latin, outer- we find ourselves left with -sad-. Now Shiant means "sacred" and is rather rare in names of the Christian period. This is actually the word which we have in the Holy Loch = An Loch Seunta and in Beinn Sianta, one of the Paps of Jura. Modern Gaelic has seun = a charm and seunta = enchanted. Perhaps—if no more than that—we have in -sad- the s + vowel + (n) = d or t of Shiant.

The two remaining names are very difficult. Malaca may be Lindisfarne— Ancient British was Medcaut and the Insenos looks suspiciously like the plural of innis = island. Possibly it is the Scillies that are intended.

Our second source is the Alexandrian geographer Ptolemy. Unfortunately he was interested mainly in the theoretic aspect of geography and he mentions names only incidentally (and it has been shown that he was not above inventing names where he lacked information). Further, his sources for Scotland were decidedly meagre. He has information for the East Coast up to Thurso, and fairly accurate information at that, and rather more doubtful information for the West Coast as far as Skye. He is vague as to the number of sea-inlets on the north side of the Clyde estuary and apparently imagines that Loch Lomond, if this is his "Gulf of Lennox", is an arm of the sea. He appears to have virtually no information for the stretch from Skye to Thurso. Apparently his information came from two separate expeditions; one up the East Coast and the other up the West.

He tells us that there are five islands which are called the Eboudai (it is a misreading of this word which gives us the word "Hebrides"). Actually, he was not so far wrong. Eboudai is the word we find in the ancient Irish tribal name Fir Iboth. This tribe of aboriginal inhabitants, whose name is not Indo-European and whose language is entirely lost, is said by Irish tradition to have been driven out of Ireland into the Scottish Isles. Here is the proof of it!

One thing we must mention. Ptolemy made a rather curious blunder. He maps Britain accurately from the South Coast to the line of the Antonine Wall (Forth–Clyde) then, no doubt through copying the error of a careless Roman Army surveyor, he turns the rest of Scotland through an angle of 90° so that the Aberdeenshire coast runs roughly East–West and the Mull of Kintyre becomes the most northerly point of the Mainland. Thus, when he speaks of East–West in Scotland, we are to understand North–South.

Here is what he actually says: "Above Ivernia (Ireland) are the islands called Eboudai, five in number. The furthest west is called Ebouda, that next to it on the east is also called Ebouda, then comes Rhicena (var. Eggarikenna), then Malios, then Epidion".

Many wild theories have been put forward to explain which islands are intended but one point is usually ignored: no sane people ever gave the same name to two large adjacent islands. Something is wrong.

Actually, as we saw above the explanation is fairly simple. The unfortunate Irish tribesmen fled before the Gael and finally they fled from Ulster into the Scottish Isles. Here we have, not the actual island names at all, but the names of the wretched refugees who had occupied them perhaps a generation or so earlier. There is really no information available so far as to which two islands these people occupied; probably archaeology will give the answer one day by a comparison of Irish and Scottish dùns but meantime either Islay and Jura or Bute and Arran would seem reasonable guesses.

The next name is obviously misplaced and cannot possibly lie immediately south of Mull. Rhicena looks like Rathlin, visible from Roman-occupied territory. The meaning is unknown. The Egga (enga(?)) should mean "near" but its use here is strange. Above it was suggested that this name matches the Sobrica of the Ravenna list and is, in fact, Eigg but it is still misplaced for the one sure landmark in Ptolemy's list is Malios = Mull.

60

Epidion has already been given by Ptolemy (correctly) as the then name for Kintyre (Árd Echde in Old Irish, with the same meaning), surely then it is odd that the same name should occur again in the North as the name of an island? This may possibly be a mistake for the island called Erimon by Ravenna. Such a mistake could actually be made fairly easily by a scribe transliterating from Latin to Greek as p in Latin uses the same symbol as r in Greek and its position would then be correct. If the name really is Epidion most probably it refers to the strategically important island of Sanda (Vinion in Ravenna) and has simply been misplaced.

Our third source is Adomnan, the biographer of St. Columba. Unfortunately he writes in Latin and this tends to mask the underlying Gaelic forms. Luckily he usually just tags on the Latin feminine ending -a to the existing name and sets it in apposition to insula (island).

Here are his names:—

Airtraig
Colosus insula
Egea   ,,
Elena   ,,
Ethica Terra
(?)Geona (perhaps this is not an island)
Hinba   insula
Hinbina   ,,
Ilea   ,,
Longa
Malea   insula
Oidech/Aithche
Ommon
Rechrea insula
Sainea   ,,
Scia   ,,

(Innis) Airtraig = Isle by the Shore was shown by Watson[4] to be the modern Shona (Ardnamurchan)-

Colosus insula may represent O.I. masc. Colos. It is mentioned in a context which makes it clear that Coll is the island intended, although that, today is a feminine word. The name has, of course, no connection with the Latin Colossus = huge. Ptolemy mentions a bay called Volsas, which may not be a bay at all but an error for Kol(s)as which again would be a masculine word. Possibly the name was originally masculine but has become feminine by analogy with other island names which are, almost without exception, feminine. The name comes from Coll = hazel and means Hazel place.

Ege(a) is Eigg (correctly) said to be from O.I. eag = a notch, with reference to the deep cutting through the centre. This, as we saw, was the place of martyrdom of St. Donnan apparently at the hands of pirates.

Elena has been dealt with before and shown to be, probably, the modern Canna.

Ethica Terra = Tir Idhe = Corn Land, i.e. Tiree.

Geon(a) is mentioned as the place from which a respectable old pagan gentleman came. Columba met him in Skye but found he could talk to him only through an interpreter. This is generally taken as evidence that Columba could not speak the language of the Picts but, on the other hand, he could well have been a member of some ancient pre-Indo-European tribe as Columba is nowhere else mentioned as having need of an interpreter. If Geon was an island (and not just a tribal name) it may have been one of the Outer Isles or even Raasay. The meaning of the word is quite unknown.

According to fairly reliable tradition, Hinb(a) is the old name of the island called Kolumbs ey = Columba's Isle by the Norse, now Colonsay. The -b- between the -m- and the -s- vanishes and the -m- becomes -n- by assimilation. The Columban monastery stood on Kiloran Bay and the ruins were plundered for the building of Colonsay House which now stands on the site[5]. The meaning of Hinb is uncertain.

There is one reference to an island called Hinbina insula, apparently Little Hinb where there was a small priory to which penitents were sent. This would appear to be the adjacent islet of Oransay = Oran's isle. When Reginald of the Isles decided to rebuild the ruins of past generations, he first set up a Benedictine monastery on the Columban site in Iona (the Columban Order was, by then, virtually dead and definitely frowned on by the Papacy) and when, rather later a House was established on Oransay, we may assume that again a pre-Norse religious site was chosen.

Ile(a) has not changed its form one whit during the 1300 years since Adomnan wrote. It is still Ile Ghorm an Fheòir—Green, grassy Islay.

I, Io is Iona. It is an ancient name and appears to be connected with the yew-tree. It was probably a pagan sanctuary in prehistoric times.

The island which in Latin may be called "Long" is impossible to identify with certainty, but probably the Long Island—Inis Fhóta is intended. There was at least one Columban site there. Adomnan presumably gives it this name as Inis Fhóta is a description rather than a true place-name.

Like Ile, Male(a) remains virtually unaltered. Muile nam Fuar-bheann Àrd, Mull of the cold, lofty peaks. The name appears to mean pre-eminent, as has been said and is most appropriate.

Aithche/Oidech as we saw in the Ravenna list is Texa. We have met it already in the list of the old divisions of Islay. The origin of the word Texa is hard to discover. It is usually explained as Norse, Bird-cherry Isle: a most improbable meaning! The ruins of the religious settlement visited by St. Coinneach of Aghabo are still in fair order. The dedication was to the Virgin Mary.

Ommon is either an error for Omon/Amon (the Ravenna Vinion), as seems most probable, or else it is a completely unknown name. There is no clue in the context to tell us anything about its position.

Rechre(a) is Rathlin.

Saine(a) is a "lost" name. As we saw, it appears in the Ravenna list as Sapona. The meaning is unknown. From the Ravenna list we deduce that it was one of the southern isles. It belonged, according to Adomnan, to the Cinel Loarn. A south wind carried Columba and his men from Saine to Iona. Leaving Saine at dawn on a summer morning they were in Iona by 9 a.m. They were, in fact, returning from Ireland and had stopped at Saine to rest. Position plus ownership narrow our choice down to Jura, for there is no other island of any size between Ireland and Iona of which we are in any real doubt as to the name and, as if to clinch the matter, we have, on the west of the island, a cave called Uamh Mhuinntir Idhe—the Cave of the Iona Party. The distance involved in travelling from that point to Iona would be slightly over thirty miles and, if it be argued that this would involve a speed of something like six miles per hour, an almost unbelievable speed for such boats, then one can reply that that is exactly the point Adomnan is making, the speed was indeed remarkable. In fact it was miraculous for this was yet another of Columba's miracles!

Scia is, of course, Skye—An t-Eilean Sgitheanach. This name appears to be connected with sgiath = a wing, but it is more than doubtful if, as has been suggested, it refers to the shape of the island. Early settlers, even if they did realise the shape of the island were a hard-headed lot, far removed from the Wingèd Isles, the Flower Dales and the Fairy Dells of Victorian times. The name probably refers to the island's protective deity who had to be kept in a good mood.

The only other name which seems to call for mention is one which appears in the Annals of Ulster. Under the year 568 A.D. mention is made that a fleet led by certain of the nobility of Dal Riada visited Sóil and Islay for plunder. The location of Sóil is a puzzle. It is usually identified with Seil because of the similarity of the names but Seil and Islay seem an oddly assorted pair. One wonders if this could be an old name for one of the islets known to-day as Eilean Nave, Eilean Orsa or Fraoch Eilean. One feels it could hardly be a scribal error for Saine, though that would be the obvious choice.

---

[1] Mod. Ellen Vannin, from Manu—the God of the Seas. Cf. Clackmannan = Manu's Stone and Slamannan (Sliabh Mhannain) = Manu's Hill.

[2] The -p- must be an error, it cannot represent an old P Celtic form.

[3] Some authorities question this. If the ascription of the poem on title page to Columba is correct, then it cannot possibly be a Norse borrowing—though the argument above still holds good.

[4] History of the Celtic Place Names of Scotland: W. J. Watson.

[5] New Stat. Acc. Jura.

CHAPTER 7

THE NORSE PERIOD

The following lines, written sometime about the mid-ninth century, set the mood of this period very well:—

Is acher ingaith innocht: fufuasna fairge findfolt.
Ni agor reimm mora minn dondlaechraid lainn ua lothlind.

Bitter is the wind tonight: it tosses the sea's white hair.
I do not fear the coursing of a clear sea by the fierce warriors from Norway.

This was a time of fear and of sudden and violent death in the Highlands such as was not known again till the years following Culloden.

THE COMING OF THE NORSE

While Scotland was growing up, stirring events were taking place elsewhere. In Norway too a nation had been developing. One of Norways' biggest problems had been solved by the mid-eighth century with the introduction of modern carpenter's tools and especially the iron axe.

For years past Norway had had to face an increasing population and unemployment problems. Foreign trade, never a major money-earner, was on the decline, farms had been sliced up so often that they were rapidly ceasing to be viable units and still the demand for land and work went on increasing. Steps were being taken: all unwanted babies were "exposed", that is, left out on the hillside to die, but this accounted for only a fraction of the surplus population.

New and sophisticated methods in carpentry helped to change all that. Now it was possible to cut planks and build proper sea-going ships. With sea-going ships, trips of exploration could be made by bold spirits: new lands could be discovered and new trading potentialities opened up. With sea-going ships people could sail away and leave poverty behind. Soon Norse ships, clinker-built to a design so excellent that it is still in use today, were carrying poor farmers from misery and squalor to at least the possibility of a new and better life.

But we are going on too fast.

It has been claimed above that the Norse overseas expansion was due to over-crowding and the iron axe. This is true but, of course, a drastic over-simplification. Perhaps it is wisest to see this period of Norse history as just one stage in the long-term movement of the Teutonic tribes which started in earnest during the 4th Century A.D. (One might then regard the great English expansion which built up the British Empire and brought about the colonisation of North America and Australasia as its final stage.)

As the tattered remains of the old Roman Empire gradually settled down to more peaceful conditions during the late seventh and early eighth centuries, opportunities for trading began to re-open. Charles Martel spent much time trying to resurrect the old North Sea coastal trade and the more northerly of the Teutons, the Scandinavians, soon began to show real interest. Round about 810 A.D. the great King Godfred of Denmark built a strong earthen wall, the Danevirke, across the neck of the Jutland Peninsula, to cut off his territories from the less happy lands between him and the Elbe, which was now the northern border of the reviving Empire. A new town Hedeby (Heath town), grew up immediately behind the Danevirke and from it a trade route developed to the Elbe and thence to the vast market of the Frankish lands. Obviously trade was now diverted away from Denmark's traditional trading partners, Norway and Sweden and they, willy-nilly, had to look outwards and abandon the old way of life. In other words, the rise of the Carolingian Empire triggered off the second stage in Teutonic expansion even as the decay of the Empire of the Caesars had triggered off the first one.

Let us look more closely at this region of Scandinavia which had now become the centre of Teutonic activity. The whole region might be compared to the roof of a house with a knife pointed to the south gable but leaning towards the east. Norway occupies the west slope, Sweden the east while Denmark is the spear, inclined towards Sweden. The ridge-pole between the first two is the Kølen (Keel), the spear-head is the Skagen with its dangerous currents. Close proximity has always made Sweden the more attractive trading partner for Denmark. To the south, of course, lies the wild Mark—the border region, cutting off Danes from Saxons.

Denmark plays a very small part in Scottish history; Danish development was southward along the coast and thence across to England. Sweden, being orientated eastwards, turned her attention to the Slavs and, eventually, to Byzantium and Baghdad. Norway, however, looked out to the empty Atlantic and had no visible means of satisfying the need for trade development. Was it this factor which made Norway lag behind the other two? The Sviar of Uppland had, by the early eighth century moulded the eastern tribes into the Swedish nation. Even as early as 800 A.D. the Danes were sufficiently well-organised to challenge the Emperor Charlemagne, but Norway remained a weak land, divided among warring chiefs. Even the very name, Norge (Norway) is almost derisive, meaning no more than "The Road North"—almost as if Scotland were to be named "The Road to England". And so we come back to the starting-point, the iron axe, which allowed Norway to take to the open sea.

The first traceable movement out of Norway is an exodus of poor farmers and cottars, probably from Hordaland, who moved to the Orkneys and Shet-lands. Whom and what they found there is hotly debated: either they killed and drove out the native population (Scottish historians), or they found the isles largely derelict through war and disease (Norwegian historians). We will never know but, having colonised these islands successfully, the Norse began to look round for other islands to occupy and the Hebrides, with a record of more than two hundred years of almost unbroken peace, were plums ripe for the plucking. First, however, the Hebrides were to be "softened up" in a rather strange manner.

Every nation has its gangsters but only Chicago and ancient Scandinavia have actually been proud of them. To be allowed to join a Norwegian gangster band, to be a Viking, was honour indeed. No one knows for sure what the word "viking" means, but nobody who had met one had any doubt as to what it stood for—bestial savagery and cruelty. Yet strangely, even cultured members of the upper strata of Norwegian society were proud to see their sons join such a band and go forth in the spring to plunder, torture and destroy, coming back in the autumn bearing money and souvenirs of the trip. The tales of Viking horrors do not bear repeating; tales of men castrated and blinded, tales of children having their brains dashed out against walls. For a Viking, to show pity was weakness, to show clemency was effeminate. One rather tough Viking had a curious foible; he disliked the practice of throwing babies into the air and catching them on spear-points. He was too tough a man for folk actually to be prepared to laugh at this but he was always known as the Bairns' Man.

Norway's early civilisation was a mass of contradictions. Hand in hand with the disgusting barbarities of the viking went the first truly democratic parliament Western Europe has known. Together with savage heathenism and the old nature gods went craftsmanship unsurpassed anywhere in the world. While the Norse were building scientifically designed vessels, the much more highly civilised Celts of Ireland and Scotland were paddling around in canoe-like boats made of wicker covered with skin.

The first recorded raid of the sort later to be known as Viking raids came in 793[1] on the little island of Lindisfarne, where the ancient Columban church and monastery were looted and burned and the surviving monks managed only with difficulty to rescue the precious relics of St. Cuthbert.

At the time it seemed that the end of the world had come. Who could have believed that the Temple of the Christian God could thus be desecrated? People recalled that, earlier in the year, portents had been seen in the sky—the opposite of the Heavenly Choir (Luke II vv 8–15)—sure sign of the coming of anti-Christ. They recalled too the horror of the clergy who had, earlier in the year, during Lent, in fact, observed drops fall from the roof of St. Peter's in York which proved, on examination, to be drops of blood.

The heathen, meantime continued, quite unabashed, to look for other likely places for plunder. The year 794 found them at Monkwearmouth, in 795 Iona went up in flames and Ireland and Wales received visits also. In 797 it was the turn of Kintyre and Man and from then until 836, which was the worst year of all, folk lived in an agony of terror. After 836 things slowly but surely improved. This was partly due to development of a sort of defensive system, partly due to the Viking movement "running out of steam"—the initial enthusiasm was gone and partly due to political developments at home in Norway.

In the mid-ninth century Harald Haarfagr seized the throne of Norway (in so far as one can be said to have existed) and proceeded to build the country up into something resembling a modern state. Inevitably he trod on many sensitive toes and the first few years of Harald's "get rough" policy were marked by a large-scale exodus of the better element of society to try to find elsewhere subjects over whom they could lord it. Most of this exodus directed itself towards the recently discovered land of Iceland—from whence the original Scottish settlers were speedily evicted.[2] On the other hand, a fair number of these dispossessed gentry made their way to the Western Isles, using the Isles as a base from which they could carry on a sort of cloak and dagger warfare against the Norwegian coast.

Harald was not the man to tolerate this sort of nonsense for long. He sent one of his generals, a man known as Ketil Flatnose (the Norse were fond of giving nicknames and this practice has lived on in the former Norse lands in Scotland) to restore law and order. Ketil worked so hard and diligently for his royal master that he established an empire which was to survive until 1462, when the last of the Isles were returned to Scotland—an empire which lasted much longer than the great British Empire. Ketil's daughter married a warrior chief called Olaf, a man whose aim in life was to seize as much territory as possible from the Scots and they two had a son called Thorstein who appears to have reigned as the effective ruler of most of Scotland north of the Great Glen. No doubt Ketil himself often visited Islay but no records survive and it is pointless to speculate on possible dwelling places he may have occupied.

It is hard indeed to get ourselves into the shoes of people who lived a thousand years ago and to understand their feelings and emotions but we can readily understand that the coming of the Norse threw the whole of Gaeldom into confusion. In Ireland especially, for hundreds of years, people had been taught that, since the coming to the land of the Christian Faith, the country was invincible. A new and bitter lesson had now to be learned when it was demonstrated the hard way that the great religious "civitates", so far from being invincible bulwarks against the heathen, were actually magnets to attract them. Durrow, Kells, Clonmacnois, Lismore and dozens of others all went up in flames. One Irishman, observing the sack of Armagh, remarked bitterly that Holy Patrick might reasonably have been expected to intervene when he saw a Norseman smashing his shrine with an axe. Why hadn't he?

The facile answer was that Ireland had erred in accepting Christianity in the first place; that the Christian God could not even defend his own sanctuaries, but that was not answer enough. It seemed that all gods must bow to the Norse. Had not the ancient and beautiful sanctuary of Aonghus a' Bhrugha (Newgrange, Co. Meath) also been desecrated and pillaged? The Vikings' own story about this was that when they broke the Neolithic seals and entered the passage, they found the god inside and that they overcame and slew him. They may not, of course, have been telling the truth.

The attitude of the native Irish was understandably confused. At times they were prepared to fight like Dervishes in the hope of driving out the invaders; at other times they not only accepted their presence, but went so far as to attempt to identify themselves with them. In moods of pessimism many Irish were inclined to say: "Both the Christian God and our own native deities have let us down. The most worthy god is therefore Thor. Let's worship him!"

The howls of woe set up by the Irish clergy about these back-sliding members of their flock are reminiscent of the Prophet Jeremiah. They coined an excellent phrase for those who had "forsaken their birthright"—the Gall-Gàidheil, the Foreign Gaels. It may be mentioned that in later years these Gall-Gàidheil became a power to be reckoned with both in Ireland and throughout the West of Scotland.

As time passed the two sides, Norse and Gael, settled down to a rather uneasy peace. Long periods of calm in an area might be followed by an outburst of violence. In aggressive mood the Irish might rise against the more defenceless of the Norse colonists, forcing them to flee for safety. It has been suggested that the Norse colony in Galloway was made up almost entirely of fugitives from Ireland and, while this is probably an exaggeration, it does seem very probable that the Norse settlements both in Galloway and Islay were made up at least as much by such refugees as by fresh colonists from the Norwegian homeland. Probably this accounts, in part at least, for the subtle differences between the place-names of Iceland which can have had few refugees from Ireland, and those of the Norse areas of Islay.

It remains only to complete this brief general summary of the Norse period before we deal with the place-names in detail. As far as Ireland was concerned the Norse power was broken early (only to be replaced by the much more serious English menace). In 1014, a certain kinglet, Brian Bóraimhe, found himself forced to turn upon the terrible Norsemen of Dublin. To the surprise of everyone, the Norse fled in disorder and from this "loss of face" they never quite recovered. When, later in the century, the warrior king, Magnus Berfott tried to restore the glories of his fathers' house, he was ambushed, overwhelmed and slain and the Norse power in Ireland was broken for ever.

In Scotland things took a rather different turn. Somehow a sense of national identity grew up in the scattered archipelago of the West. Somehow a kingdom emerged. A kingdom vassal to Norway and, later, coming to form part of the Norwegian bishopric of Trondheim, but nevertheless a real kingdom with a very real sense of nationality. The folk of the Isles, in fact, came to think of themselves, not as either Scots or Norse, but as Islesmen. It is easier, of course, to build up such a spirit than to break it down again and the "nationalism" of the Isles continued to be a thorn in the Scots' kings' sides until the seventeenth century when the last remnants of the old Kingdom were smashed in a singularly bloody manner.

During the course of the eleventh century there arose in Islay a certain nobleman of the Rhinns (Norse, of course), called Godred Crovan. This man was to leave his mark on history. Godred believed that the Isles should hive off from Norway and Scotland and establish themselves as a sovereign state: he himself was quite prepared to take on the job of king. Exactly what his qualifications were is a little obscure, but he certainly did succeed in uniting Gael and Norse in a common cause. The affection with which his name is still remembered in the Highlands is proof of that. Initially Godred seems to have had a run of luck but, unfortunately for him, that ghastly man Magnus Berfott now came to the throne in Norway (1093–1103). Magnus had grown up with an almost fanatical pride in the traditions of Norse glory yet, wherever he looked, it seemed that Norse power was being eroded. With a zeal worthy of better causes, Magnus set himself the task of rebuilding the old Empire of the Norse and so zealously indeed did he labour that he ensured that, as far as the Isles at least were concerned, whatever form of government they might get in the future, they would not have Norse government. From his time on, the Isles paid no more than a sullen lip-service to the Norse kings. Magnus' method of regaining respect was to go through the Isles, looting and plundering each in turn—his biographer tells us that he "left smoke over Islay". Indeed the Outer Isles and Islay seem to have suffered most. Magnus made two great raids and, as has been said, during the latter he was ambushed and killed while administering Jedburgh Justice to the Irish.

Godred, deposed by Magnus, evidently lived out his life in obscurity and was buried, according to a tradition we have no reason to doubt, near Kintra Farm, Port Ellen, where his grave is marked by a large stone. The stone itself has acquired a Gaelic name, Carragh Bàn = Fair Obelisk, but the ridge above still has the Gaelic/Norse name Druim an Stun G. Ridge of the N. Stone.

After the assassination of Magnus, Godred's son, Olaf Kleining, took the Throne of the Isles and reigned without let or hinderance over the whole area, making Man his capital. A story is told concerning this period. It is said that every year Olaf's galley came to Islay to collect the rents and that it anchored in the North Bay, Port Ellen. People paying in money went to the rock opposite the present Ramsay Hall, which is still known as Creag an Airgid (Money Rock) while those paying in kind went to the rock on which the distillery now stands and it is called Creag nan Nithean (Rock of the Articles).

Olaf married Elfrica[3], the daughter of Fergus, the last monarch of a semi-independent Galloway and, incidentally, great-great-great grandparent of Robert the Bruce.

There follows a rather complicated story.

Olaf had a son, Godred, and a daughter Ragnhildis, and when, after a long and prosperous reign, he died, his son ascended the throne of a reasonably happy and contented kingdom. He thereupon set to work to undo all his father's work by sheer stupidity. Meantime, his sister had married an enigmatic character, called by the Norse name of Somerled. An unusual, but not unique name. From this marriage came two of Scotland's leading families, the MacDonalds and the MacDougalls, as well as several lesser ones.

It is obviously unthinkable that two such typically Scottish families should actually be Norse and not of Scottish origin at all. Something had to be done about it and done it was by the Clan Donald bards and the pseudo-historians of a later date. They declared that, although Somerled was admittedly a Norse name, Somerled's father had borne the good old Gaelic name of Gille-Bhrìde and that, in fact, the two had been the bane of the Norse, fighting bitterly against them in order to get the Isles restored to Scotland. This inherently improbable claim has been accepted uncritically by modern historians who ignore the fact that no less a person than a Norse king considered Somerled a suitable person to accept into his, a noble Norse family. Hardly likely if Somerled had been anti-Norse! Further ignored is the admitted fact that, far from trying to restore the Isles to Scotland, Somerled ended his days by declaring war on Scotland and getting himself killed during a pointless raid on Strathclyde.

Meantime, however, when the nobility of the Isles realised that to continue under Godred's rule was impossible, they approached Somerled and asked him if he would be agreeable to having his eldest son, Dughall, placed on the throne instead of his uncle. Somerled agreed and espoused his son's cause with such vigour that the news of what was happening soon reached Godred's ears. Somerled found himself in a very nasty position when Godred's battle-fleet sailed north to deal with him.

Somerled was lucky. After an indecisive battle in the Sound of Jura (1156), Godred sued for peace. Somerled and Godred divided the Isles between them: Somerled got everything south of Ardnamurchan except Man, while Godred retained the rest. There was now no word of Dughall becoming king.

After Somerled's death the kingdom was again divided among his sons. Dughall, the eldest, from whom the MacDougalls are descended, getting Lorne and the adjacent isles; Reginald, the MacDonald's ancestor, getting Islay and Aonghus, the youngest, getting most of what was left. The line of Reginald quickly established the precedence of Islay, the MacDougalls helping in the process by taking the wrong side during the Wars of Independence and refusing to admit their error even when it was obvious that Scotland would re-gain her liberty. The MacDonalds' hold over Islay and the Isles survived until finally smashed during the seventeenth century. Here is a little table to have in mind:—

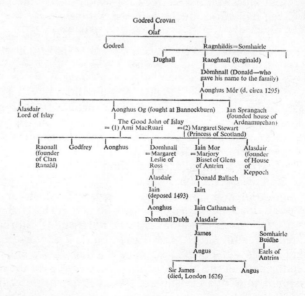

Notes: There is some doubt as to whether Alasdair reigned for a while after Aonghus Mór or whether Aonghus Òg succeeded directly. The Macvurich historians who compiled the Clanranald Manuscript say that Aonghus Mór died in 1234 and Aonghus Og in 1306 but these dates are certainly wrong. Aonghus Og was at Bannockburn in 1314 and his father was probably alive at the time of the Battle of Largs (1263).

The Good John of Islay was the man who inspired the phrase: "You could have fooled me". His first marriage was to his wealthy cousin Amy MacRuari. He had three sons by her, in addition to her money. He then cynically discarded her, disinherited his children, and made an even better marriage to the Princess Margaret Stewart, daughter of the king. Latterly he became senile and it was Reginald, his disowned son, who had to take charge of the affairs of the Lordship. This job he carried out with great efficiency, proving both clever and popular. To the dismay of the magnates of the Isles, as soon as his half-brother came of age, he insisted on carrying out his dead father's wishes and handing the Lordship over to him. He really seems to have been a most exceptional man and his descendants, deservedly came to be among the most respected of the Siol Dòmhnaill. It is believed that he is buried in the Church of St. Mary on Texa.

In spite of misgivings, Dòmhnall too proved to be a most excellent leader and it may be said that the House of Islay reached its zenith under him. The Clan Donald administered territories which stretched from the borders of Caithness in the north to quite near Belfast in the south and constituted a threat of terrifying proportions to the Scottish monarchy, weakened by the kidnapping of King James I by English pirates. The only real attempt to contain MacDonald power made by the Regent Albany ended in the disastrous battle at Harlaw in 1411 and in Albany's eventual execution. Sitting on the jury which condemned him to death was the Lord of the Isles! Truly, for a time Finlaggan was a real capital city.

The rot set in under Alasdair (1425–1449). He was no general and some rather aimless military manoeuvres of his, undertaken with no very obvious end in view, ended in the degrading spectacle of his kneeling before the King and Court, naked, to plead for clemency. From this humiliation the Isles never fully recovered. Several absurd rebellions were now undertaken both by Alasdair and his son John and these suited Edinburgh very nicely, giving just the required excuse for action against an over-powerful and over-ambitious family. In 1493, James IV, posing as the honest and reasonable man who has explored every avenue and found no other solution, at last acted. He abolished the Lordship altogether. The bungling John, Lord of the Isles, already distracted by his quarrel with an illegitimate son who, Absalom-like had roused the subjects against his father, died the following year. This son, Aonghus, had married a daughter of the Earl of Argyll by whom he had a son, Donald. When Aonghus was murdered at Inverness a year or two later, the Earl seized the opportunity to put an end to the Lordship once and for all. He seized the infant and imprisoned him in Innischonnel on Loch Awe. This is one of the blackest marks against the Campbell family as most of his life was to be spent in prison.

Meanwhile, lest it be felt that James acted unreasonably in getting rid of John MacDonald, it is worth pointing out that in 1462, this John entered into a secret agreement with Edward IV of England in which the two agreed to attack Scotland simultaneously from West and South and divide the country between them.

Following the failure of the main line, the leadership passed to the Dùn Naomhaig family, the line of Iain Mór Tàinisdear, second son of Margaret Stewart. This very interesting family restored, for a time, the family greatness and doings at Lagavullin were a matter of concern in European capitals. The family held great influence in Ireland on account of their vast estates there and, at a time when Elizabeth of England was quarrelling with Spain, she could ill afford to quarrel with the Irish magnates. It is said, on rather vague authority, that one of the daughters of the House, known locally as the Inghean Dubh—Dark-haired Daughter, proposed that the men, with their continual petty bickering, should stand aside and let the women drive the English out of Ireland. It is said that her plan was to bring Irish troops over to the family hunting-grounds on Jura, train them in guerrilla warfare and send them back to Ireland to carry out harrying raids. If this old story is correct, it is well worth noting that she simply foresaw the plan which Michael Collins was to use successfully in the twentieth century—though he was unable to use Jura as a training-ground!

The two Iains, father and son, named on the family tree, contrived to quarrel with the Government and were hanged together on the Burghmuir in Edinburgh. Angus sold the estates to Campbell of Cawdor and then regretted his bargain. Force was finally used to eject him and James was held in Edinburgh as surety for the good behaviour of the Isles. A letter written during this period by the gentleman farmers of Islay is one of our most useful sources of the farm-names. James escaped from custody, made his way home and seized Dùn Naomhaig. The island rose for him but, of course, a small detachment of soldiers soon settled the rebellion. Sir James fled from Port na haven (1616) for Spain. In due course he made his way to London where the English Government granted him a state pension. He died in the White Tower in 1626.

It would appear that Sir James retained the farms of Ardilistry and Cnoc Raonasdail and that these were eventually sold by his heirs. The money gained was used to purchase the lands of Tannelmuir (Renfrewshire) which remained in the family until the nineteen sixties.

From Somhairle Buidhe, another son of Alasdair of Dùn Naomhaig were descended the Earls of Antrim.

Dun Naomhaig's last hour of glory came during the Montrose campaigns when Alasdair MacColla seized the ancestral family home and set a garrison in it under his father, Colla Ciotach. Colla surrendered (or came out under a flag of truce, the facts are uncertain) to the Earl of Argyll who promptly seized and hanged him. Either to this period or to the earlier Islay rebellion belongs the name Bealach nam Marbh on the opposite side of the bay. This is, beyond doubt, the spot where the "smaller fry" of the uprising were gibbeted. Alasdair himself, the last of the great MacDonalds, retreated to Irish soil to continue the fight and was eventually slain at Cnoc nan Dos (Co. Cork) in 1647.

One last thing to notice before we end this summary is the change of language. Olaf's family is obviously Norse-speaking, Somerled's children appear to have a mixture of Norse and Gaelic names but from then on the Norse names virtually disappear. Since Somerled was killed in 1164 and since we can take it that he, as a nobleman, would be a leader of fashion, it would appear that the decline of the Norse tongue started, say, three generations before the Battle of Largs.

Part 2

It is fairly easy to trace out the main lines of Norse settlement in Islay since the numbers involved were relatively small. It is much harder in, say, Lewis, where the bulk of the settlement names are of Norse origin. Although what follows is, in a sense conjecture, it is still reasonably safe conjecture.

Probably the first Norse names to be given were names of natural features seen from the sea, i.e. sailors' names. Imagine ships approaching Islay from the north. The first sight of land is the headland of Rudha a' Mhàil. Now this name translates as Gaelic = Headland of the tax, said to refer to a tax the Clan Donald is alleged to have levied on shipping passing through the Sound. It could, however, equally well be Gaelic Rudha prefixed to the Norse Fjall = mountain. If mhail does = fjall then the original name would be Fjalls nes = Mountain headland, which would fit very well.

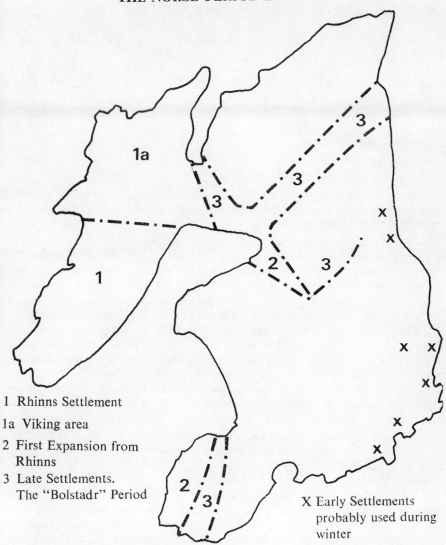

1 Rhinns Settlement

1a Viking area

2 First Expansion from Rhinns

3 Late Settlements. The "Bolstadr" Period

X Early Settlements probably used during winter

Having reached Islay, which they re-named Il, the natural route to follow then was down the Sound of Islay (Norse. Ilar Sund; Gaelic. Caol Ile), between Islay and Jura. Jura is itself a Norse name, Dýr ey = Deer/wild animal island, and this replaces the older name which was probably (though not certainly) Saine. Passing down the Sound, both sides have Norse names for prominent features. Here are just a few:—

Il = Islay

Araig = Àr vík (Bonnahaven) River harbour

Margadail = (?) Market dale

(Port) Askaig = Ask vík = Ashtree harbour[5]

Boreraig = Borgar vík = Fort harbour

(Gleann) Garrasdail = Gerðis dalr = personal name = dale

(Gleann) Choireadail—apparently a borrowing from G. coire = cauldron referring to its shape + dale

Dýr ey = Jura

(Gleann) Asdail = Áss dalr = Ridge dale

Daimhsgeir = Dauf sker = Blunt skerry[4]

(Gleann) Ullibh—meaning doubtful. Possibly = wolf, more probably a personal name

Brosdal = personal name + dale[6]

(Camus an) Staca = (Bay of the) Stack (rock column)

(Rudha nan) Tràille = þraella nes = Slave promontory

Notice here how a later generation who did not understand Norse added Gleann, Port, etc. so that Port Askaig really means Harbour of Ash-tree harbour. This is called tautology.

Those names, given by sailors, reflect the interests of sailors. Among all the Norse names we will be looking at on the east side of Islay there is not one case where the generic element is a word meaning "farm" or "estate" or anything of the kind. On the contrary, we find bay, harbour, dale, reef, and so on.

Even sailors must come ashore sometime, however, and very probably the first Norse settlements on the island included Proaig, Trùidirnis, Àros and Glais Uig. The first, Proaig, is just Breiðr vík = Broad harbour/bay (as in Brodick), Àros = Áross = River mouth[7], Glais Uig = Glaes (nom. glaer) vík = Sea harbour, but Trùidirnis = Trúidir nes is more difficult. Nes is just N.[8] a headland and on the headland in question lies one of the small vitrified forts discussed above. In all probability the Norse learned this name from the local people and rendered it into the Norse sounding genitive "trúj + ir". There is no such word as trūj in either Gaelic or Norse and this is, in fact, a relic of a lost language.

Having once landed, the next move was obviously to expand inland and this our Norse sailors proceeded to do. Proaig, by its very nature was unsuitable for expansion, but the Trùidirnis-Àros colony expanded quite a bit. Kintour itself is Gaelic in form = Tower Head and may, just possibly, refer to the dùn, Dùn a' Mhullaich Bhuidhe, on the hill opposite. On the other hand, it may equally well be the gaelicised form of some older name. One can't help but notice the similarity: trū(j) -tūr (n.b. in both cases the vowel is long). It is a strange co-incidence that the vowel -u-, uncommon in local names should occur in adjacent farms. Could this Trūj be an old district name? It is worth mentioning that in many cases where the Norse names do not admit of an easy translation the probable reason is that we are actually dealing with an ancient name in Norse dress. Ancient languages were spoken in Scotland down to the time of Columba at least. Why, for example, should the Norse call Lewis "Poets' house" or anything of the sort? It doesn't make sense!

To resume. Alongside Kintour Farm is Tallant, probably Hall-lendi = the Slope, which describes it very well (though some claim that this name is ancient

Gaelic being the same as Tailtiu). The general, though not universal, rule is that an initial Norse h- becomes t- in Gaelic as such words are normally regarded as masculine and this allows them to become pronounceable in Gaelic by prefixing the Definite Article, an t-. Tallant is Talanda in Gaelic.

The Norse followed both the Claigeann and Kintour rivers upstream. They named the former Leir á (G. Leòra—Muddy River)—the upper section runs through Gleann Leòra and this gives the clue, but their name for the Kintour River is lost. That they did penetrate upstream here is shown by the tiny settlement at Staoin, under the shadow of the Iron Age fort, Dùn Fhinn. Presumably their name for this fort was Stein borg because staoin = stein, a stone.

Further along the coast they landed at the little bay called Loch a' Chròic and apparently met organised opposition. Tradition tells of a savage battle fought here between the "Danes" and the locals which ended, like all good battles, with the invaders being driven off and their leader left slain. Our story brings with it a sort of bonus because the leader was a giantess! Her name was Ela (from which, the old folk maintained, the island name was derived though how, I never could see) and she was buried between two standing-stones at the top of the brae.

Actually the Norse appear to have made regular use of this bay as the names show. They must also have been a real nuisance, as the road linking the N.E. and S.W. parts of the parish runs along the shore at this point. No wonder the locals attacked them! Loch a' Chròic is a part translation of Króks vík = Curve bay[9]; (Cnoc) Raonasdail = Reynis dalr = Rowan dale; Tobar a Lì is a part translation of Brynnr a hlíf = the Well from the Cliff (this is a very ancient well recognised as the half-way point between the two parts of the parish). The steep hill beyond the well, site of the battle, is (Bruthach) Sheònish = Sjó nes = Sea point. Beyond this again lies (Aird) Thorr-innis. Now it is certainly tempting to see Thor's ness in this name, especially as it occurs so close to a "rowan" name and Thor was fond of the rowan. Further, the same name occurs in the Rhinns at a place where Thor was certainly worshipped. Alas, it will not do! þors nes could not give Torr-innis and this is probably no more than a ness belonging to Thori.

The existence of all these names suggests that the Norse had a nice, snug little hide-out at Loch a' Chròic and that although the locals resented this, they just had to make the best of it.

The next name down the coast is at Lagavullin Bay, Surneig, which, in spite of difficulties with the phonetics, is almost certainly the "Dirty, muddy neck of land". Behind Lagavullin rises Solum = Sauði holmr = Sheep hill.

Next comes Laphroaig. The meaning of this is obscure to me, but it is, presumably related in some way to Proaig. There is an old story of a battle fought from Proaig to Laphroaig (Latha Phroaig) but it will not do!

Then we have Leodamus, the old name for Port Ellen = Leod's moss. It is still in use as the name of the bay[10]. Finally we have Stremnish (Straum-nes) = Current ness.

We can regard this Kildalton settlement as one suitable for wintering or as occasion might demand, rather than a place of permanent settlement and the first real, indeed the main settlement in Islay was made elsewhere: in the Rhinns. Here was an area virtually separated from the rest of Islay, much more so than now-a-days for the Moine Mhór, the Big Bog, at the head of Loch Gruineirt was then, and continued into the nineteenth century, almost impassable swamp. The crossing places were at Uisge an t-Suidhe where one could cross with reasonable safety (the river was much smaller then) but over yards of loose gravel, or else over the Gruineart sands.

In the southern part of the Rhinns the list of the farm names reads almost like a portion of the Landnámabók—the book which tells of the settlement of Iceland. The Rhinns must, in fact, have been almost entirely Norse-speaking after the settlement and life must, indeed have been hard for the few Gaels remaining. Strangely, however, the churches seem to have remained unmolested —or the major ones at least. The names Kilchoman and Kilchiaran would have disappeared from memory had there not been a continuing Gaelic-speaking priesthood there, as would Baile an Aba (Balinaby = the Abbot's township) which remains to this day, surrounded by Norse names.[11]

What was life like for the faithful few who remained? The beaches below Kilchoman Kirk were certainly used by the Vikings—though the Rhinns Viking colony seems to have been confined to this corner. What were the emotions of the priest at the altar of the church as the heathen streamed past his door bearing their plunder? What invisible barrier existed between Norse and Gael? These are unanswerable questions. We can, however, say that most of the Rhinns settlers were not Vikings but farmers, and farmers, except when their stock or their fields are threatened, are men of peace. We may assume that, after the initial seizures of land from the Gaels, when the Norse farmers had established themselves, they would ask only to be left in peace and quiet and the Viking would be discouraged from terrorising the local population whether Gael or Norse.

At the time of the settlement of the Isles and Iceland, the names for a farm in common use were "staðr" and the less common "bólstaðr", both having roughly the same social status; "setr", a smaller farm, and the word "boer", rapidly passing out of use, which had come to mean an estate rather than a farm (the reason being that the old "boers" had all been sliced up so many times since they were first established as farms that "boer" had come to be thought of as a piece of land far too big for any ordinary man to own). When we examine the numerical frequency of these names in the Rhinns we find that it is much the same as is found in Iceland. We have one "boer", appropriately a king's "boer"; five, or perhaps more "staðr's", two "bólstaðr's" and one "setr".

From the Landnámabók mentioned above we can see that it was the fashion of the time to name a farm after its owner, i.e. the descriptive element is usually a personal name. This is subject, of course, to the qualification that the higher one goes in the social scale the less likely it is for the farm to be called after the owner since the farm of the most important person in the area would tend to be just "*The* Farm" and would not need further description. We can mention here

76

that in Islay at least, the "bólstaðr" tended to be slightly more important than the "staðr". Further, as we shall see, it was to survive longest as a living word.

Boer:	Conisby	—Konungs Boer	—King's Estate[12]
Bólstaðr:	Bolsa	—	—Farm (unqualified)
	Nerabus	—Nedri Bólstaðr	—Nether farm[13]
Staðr:	Cultorsa	—? þoris staðr with Kúla = a knoll[14]	—The hillock of Thori's farm
	Glassansa	—? staðr	—? farm (West end of Port Charlotte)
	Greamsa	—Grims staðr	—Grim's farm
	Olista	—Olafs staðr	—Olaf's farm
	Kelsa	—Kjalar staðr[15]	—Keel farm
Setr:	Eresaid	—Eriks setr	—Erik's smallholding

Apart from the farm names surprisingly few Norse names have survived: minor place-names do tend to be ephemeral—a new tenant moving into a farm may rename the fields and even give new names to hills, glens, etc. if the existing names are unknown to him or are in a strange language. The farm name itself tends to survive. This is because the incoming tenant has contracted to occupy the farm known as x or y and so all parties are agreed on what the name is. In this way we have preserved such names as Tormisdale = Tormods dalr = Norman's dale[16]; Cladville, which has already been dealt with; Amot = A mot = River junction, and so on, which had become the names of actual farms.

It is, however, worth pointing out that, even in the Rhinns where Norse settlement was most dense, some Gaels did continue to live on their farms. Indeed it would seem that few farmers were actually evicted, though they did have land confiscated. This can be shown in two ways. First, we have Gaelic names such as Octomore and Octofad which clearly belong to the earlier days of Gaelic settlement, when the original bailtean were being sub-divided and secondly, the value of the baile was reckoned to be ten marks (£6 . 13/4d or £6 . 66⅔p) and if we add up the values of the farms with Gaelic names they work out at roughly ten marks for each parish—the valuation was not reduced!

Here are some topographical names which have survived, though some seem to be very corrupt:—

Hillnames:—

(Beinn) Tart a' Mhill = Hjartar fjall = Hart fell
(Cnoc) Garbh a' Mhill = (?) Gørvi fjall + Hill of supplies
(„) Bhi-bhuirn = (?) Mið brynnr = The well in the middle
(„) Ung-reek-in = Ongr Hrygg-in = Narrow-ridge hill
(„) Undail = Hund dalr = Dog dale. This same name occurs as Tundal, a more regular borrowed form, in Kildalton Parish.

Skerry names:—

Crois sgeir = Kross sker = Cross skerry
Mias sgeir = Mjott sker = Narrow skerry

Tannais sgeir = Hatt nes sker = High ness skerry (actually it is low ground
with a little boss on the promontory but the accuracy of the translation is
confirmed by the Gaelic name of the promontory: Rudha na h-Àirde Móire
= Point of the High Ness

Islet:—

(Eilean) Orsay = (probably) Christian Norse: St. Oran's Isle.

Norse harbour names are very rare in the Rhinns. This can only mean that
the Norse settlers had turned their back on the sea and were concentrating on
farming.

For some reason the farms at the north end of the Rhinns do not fit into
the same general pattern. Possibly the viking and sea-faring element was stronger
there. There are many traces of viking activity along the sandy beaches of the
north-west and a number of good archaeological finds have been made. Unfortunately when the name of a farm does not contain the generic element for
"farm" or "dwelling", it makes it rather hard to tell which came first, the farm
or the name. If, for example we find a farm called Port an t-Sruthain = Stream
Bay, we have to ask ourselves if somebody came along and built a farm on a
previously unnamed piece of ground and then said; "I will call my new farm
Port an t-Sruthain" or, as we happen to know happened in the case of the Islay
farm of this name, did he come to a place known for generations as Port an
t-Sruthain and build a farm at that place.

This might seem a minor point but a moment's thought will show that such
farms as Graineil, Tormisdale and the like, although they bear Norse names,
might actually have been built by Gaels at a much later date and have no real
connection with the Norse settlement. It is often quite impossible to say whether
or not such a name started life actually as a farm name or merely as a topographical term. One example of a topographical name being adapted for a later
farm is Croisprig. This is Norse, Kross brekka = Cross slope and obviously
refers to the sandy slope running from the sea up to the (ancient) Kilchoman
cross (near the War Graves)—it is, in fact the Norse name for the area round
Tràigh a' Mhachaire. The later builder simply utilised the old name, although it
is quite inappropriate at the site of the steading and, of course, has not the
remotest connection with the so-called Dùn Chroisprig, the original name of
which has been lost.

Perhaps the easiest way to consider this area is to go round it as a Norse
tax-collector might have, starting from the Gaelic site, Goirtean and going up
the hill along the ancient road past Foreland (For-lendi = Land between sea and
hills), skirt the moor to Sunderland (apparently Hinterland with Islay's prothetic s-[17]. The road continues on to Croisprig and Coul = Kúla = Knob, round
hill and so north by Saligo to Smaull. Saligo is probably Sela gja = Seal creek,
though one would not have expected the -e- of sela to give -a-, while Smaull is
Smá hlíð[18] = the Little Cliff. This cliff is a most distinctive feature; a mass of
Torridonian rock, rough and craggy, standing out like a pillar. The ness at
Smaull is Lamanis = Hlad hamar nes = Piled up rock ness.

The road now turns inland to skirt the north end of Loch Gorm (its Norse name is lost) and we come to a puzzling name, Grùlin. This name occurs also in Mull and in Skye, but no satisfactory explanation of it has so far been given. Similarly Braigo, lying behind it, is rather obscure. It appears to mean Broad creek, but it lies a mile from the sea. I suggest that this name originally referred to the creek at Sannaig but was felt to be a suitable name for the farm when it was built (it is not ancient). At Sannaig we are, paradoxically, on firm ground, for this is certainly Sand vík = Sandy bay, an excellent harbour for Norse-type ships and even to-day, movement of the sand dunes can reveal traces of long digested dinners round the camp-fire. It is hardly surprising that Norse names survive for several prominent features along the lee approach shore:—

Sleidmeall = Sletta fjall = Hill of the plain or Slettr fjall = smooth hill (the more probable one).

Muirnemeall = (?) Myrr . . . Fjall = Bog . . . Hill.

Langadail = Langr dalr = Long dale—obvious when you have walked it!

(Tràigh & Eilean) Nòstaig = Aust vík = East harbour i.e. East from the ships passing it.

Boghachan (Móra) = G. plural of N. Boði = a breaker and hence, the reef on which it breaks.

N.B. N. Fjall is often confused in place-names with G. meall = a heap.

Returning to the main road and continuing towards the east we have:—

Gruineart = Grunnd fjördr = Shallow loch.

Graineil = Groenn völlr = Green meadow.

(?) Aoradh = possibly Eyrar vagr = Gravel-bank bay but in Gaelic it is Bruthach an Aoraidh which is explained locally as the Slope of the Adoration=it faces eastwards and it is conjectured that the druids may have worshipped the rising sun at this place. There certainly are traces of an ancient temple nearby—a site almost completely destroyed during the last war.

Development of the original settlement

Not all historical data is given on the authority of the holy saints, but it so happens that we have the word of St. Columba for the fact that he left Ireland from Lough Foyle and, when one looks into it, one finds he could not have chosen a better spot. The waters of the North Channel are called Sruth na Maoile in Gaelic, the Stream of the Mull, and the name is apt: there are many more comfortable places than the channel between Ireland and Kintyre on a stormy day. To think of braving these waters in an Irish curragh made of wicker and skin makes one's blood run cold! Out of this awful area of currents and overfalls there is one easy run: Lough Foyle to Lochindaal. It would appear, in fact, that Lochindaal was the focal point for a trade-route which ran from Ireland, overland to Port Askaig, by ferry to Jura and thence, from Lagg or Ceann Uachdrach to Loch Sween and Crinan Harbour. Lochindaal is named from the farm

Dàil, once the centre of the island. Dàil is a difficult word to translate but here it means a focal point. Although the connection with Ireland has long been severed, the route from Islay, through Jura, to the Mainland continued in regular use until last century by the cattle drovers.

An ancient traveller would find his curragh blown straight across from Lough Foyle by the prevailing south-west wind to Lochindaal. He could then choose, according to the weather and his ultimate destination, whether to risk the Mull of Oa or Rhinns Point or to take the safer road by foot through the strath to Port Askaig. The importance of this trade-route was to affect the Norse plans for expansion.

The Rhinns is a relatively fertile area: far more fertile than most of Norway. It is also isolated and, as we saw, relatively safe for an unwarlike community; far more so than an Ireland beginning to recover from the invasion of the foreigners. More and more Norsemen made their way to the Rhinns until room had to be found for this "explosion" of population. The possibility of expansion across the bog at Gruineart must have been considered, but does not seem to have been followed up immediately. I would suggest that this was because the opposition of the Gaels to a possible severing of the trade-route was likely to make things too hot in that quarter! The evidence suggests that other measures were tried.

Across, eastwards from the Rhinns, lies the wild barren peninsula called the Oa. It is roughly circular, with a north-south watershed and cliff-girt. The cliffs on the west are pierced here and there by the ends of glens which run up towards the central spine. The rocks are mainly phyllites overlaid with peat. This area had, of course, long been settled by the Gael but it was of little economic importance. This was the area the Norse decided to "clear". Landing at the foot of each of these western glens, they attempted to push the older population eastwards over the "spine".

The first glen ran up behind the Celtic farm called Kintra, which was evidently avoided. Behind the farm is (Port) Alsaig = apparently, the Harbour with the Slope (The land rises steeply from the shore). From this harbour, the glen running east was called, probably, Frakki's dalr (Frakki's dale) G. Frachdal (the other possibility is that this is a Norse attempt at the Gaelic "fraoch" = heather). Further up the glen is the obscure Uigeasgaig = ? + strip of land (Wgasgog in 1408). Possibly Viga's strip.

The next glen south was given the name Gras dalr—G. Grasdal = Grassy glen and an old religious centre was taken over and given the name Hauka holmr—G. Tocamol = Hawks' holm.

The third glen had a prominent ridge running down the centre and this was named Áss dalr—G. Glen Asdal = Ridge dale. Two farms Upper and Lower Glen Asdal, were established here at an early date and there is a third one between called Torrnabakin, which is the Norse Bakki-nn = the Bank or Cliff with the Gaelic word of similar meaning prefixed. This steading lies under a rather fearful cliff of Mull of Oa phyllites. Strangely "bakin" is made feminine (na Gaelic gen. sing. Fem. of the Definite Article) although the Norse is Masculine.

The last glen before the Mull was "cleared" only on its north slope. The farm on the south slope remains as Cill' Eathain = St. John's Church. In this glen we have Gil—G. Giol = a Gully and further up the glen we have a steading called Fangdu. Now there is a Gaelic word "fang" meaning a sheep-fold but this cannot be it because "fang" is a feminine word and would have given us "Fang Dhubh". The position of the steading tells us that we have here the Norse word "vangr" = a field with the suffixed Gaelic adjective "dubh" = black, dark.

At this stage the Gaels still held at least half the Oa: all the land to the east of the watershed and odd corners to the west of it. In addition to Kintra and Cill' Eathain, they probably held the upper part of Glen Asdal. At anyrate the upper part is still called by the old Gaelic name Gleann Gobhlach—the Forked Glen, and this was probably the pre-Norse name for the whole glen. We can leave the Oa for a while and look at another small settlement which was probably more or less contemporaneous.

To the south-east of Bridgend lies a hill and steading known by the Gaelic names Cnoc and Gart Loist—The Burnt Hill and Garden and there are vague traditions of a battle between Gaels and Norse having taken place about here (cf. the works of the Islay bard, William Livingstone). Round this area there settled a little band of Norse who have left a cluster of names to mark their passing. There is one "boer"—Neriby, which is probably Knorr's boer—(It is not the same -e- as in Nerabus. There is one "bólstaðr", Grobolls = perhaps Groa's bólstaðr—this name occurs in the Landnámabók, and there are a few topographical names.

Near the point at which they must have landed, an old track, now the B 8016, runs off into the hills, emerging eventually near Port Ellen. Near the point at which it crosses the Laggan, a branch leads off through a broad glen, and emerges at Ballygrant. We can follow the advance of the Norse up these two roads by the narrow line of Norse names. On the unclassified "Glen" road the Norse names gradually peter out but they continue almost without a break right down to Port Ellen, showing that there was at least some contact between the Gartloist and the Oa settlements, even though it was by a tenuous line through the moors for as far as I can see, there are no Norse names between the B 8016 and the sea south of Bowmore until one reaches Glenegidale, (?) Bataichean Bàna and Frachdale.

Obviously this settlement did not thrive. It was too isolated and too vulnerable to attack by the Gaels.

Here are the names:—

Neriby—Knorr's boer.

Grobolls—Groa's bólstaðr.

Scouller = Kúler—the Knolls, with prothetic s-.

Tallant = (?) N. Hatt land—High land.

          (?) N. Ha lenda—similar meaning

          (?) G. Unknown meaning.

Continuing up the so-called Glen Road, we have:—

Nòsbrig—A most unusual fort and its name presents some difficulties. The first element appears to mean "hill" (not "turf" as stated in some texts) but the second element is doubtful. As a general rule "-brig" is from "brekki", a slope, but locally it is believed to mean "fort", in which case it is a form of "borg" showing metathesis. The older forms are: Nawysporge (1509), and Navisborge (1499) which would suggest "borg", but Nosbrig (1686) gives the modern pronounciation.

(Cnoc) Cro a' Mhail—probably Rauna fjall—Rough Hill. Its south face is craggy and rather unlike the surrounding area.

(Cnoc) Amanta—Confluence. (+ G. Hill).

Cattadale—Katta dalr—Cat Glen (Katta is the gen. pl. of Köttr). Does this mean that there were wild cats in Islay then, or is it the trace of an older, tribal name?

(Beinn and Loch) Bharradail (better Mharradail) = Mark dalr—Boundary dale. And, of course, there are no further Norse names beyond this point (Borreraig is not part of this group, having taken its name from the harbour below). I was told that this name meant "boundary" by a local gamekeeper who certainly knows no old Norse.

Barr (farm) is doubtful. The farm stands on a little knoll and the Gaelic "Barr", a summit is the obvious meaning. On the other hand, the ridge running between it and Loch Bharradail is Maol a' Bharra and it may be that "Barr" has been formed from "Barradail" through a misunderstanding of its meaning after the close of the Norse period (popular etymology).

Continuing along the road towards Port Ellen we have:—

Torra—apparently Horn á—the River of the corner. The steading lies in a right angle formed by the Duich River[19].

(Gleann) Egidale—Eik dalr—Oak dale—the oaks are still there. We can be sure that this is not a name given by sailors like similar names on the Sound of Islay, since the oaks are out of sight of the sea and we today see this area almost as the Norse saw it.

Next comes a Gaelic name, Airigh Mhaol-Chaluim, which is probably pre-1000 A.D. but it is followed by:

Laorin—Leira-n—the Mud flat.

(Druim) Sgaraba—perhaps from "skarpr"—barren.

The Third Step

Political boundaries are, at best, ephemeral things and, even when things were at their worst, there must have been a certain amount of come and go between the Gaels and the Norse. Cattle cannot distinguish between Celtic grass and Norse grass and so, even such a little thing as a straying cow could lead to intercourse between the races. To maintain a permanent armed militia to guard internal Islay frontiers was an impossibility for either side and, willy-nilly, farmers had to meet to discuss livestock, cropping, march dykes and other matters of common interest. Again, it must have been a difficult and thankless task trying to keep the young folk from playing together and forming friendships. Such friendships end all too often in marriages and, in spite of all the hymns of hate sung by Gael against Norseman, such marriages did take place. The older folk just had to make the best of it!

Besides this Norse and Gael did have things to offer each other. For example, the Gaelic "marine" vocabulary is rich in Norse words and this is most easily explained by supposing that Gaels apprenticed their sons to Norse ship-wrights—indeed it is hard to see any other way in which it could have happened. At any rate, thanks to the Norse, for the first time ever, Gaels were able to build and travel in proper sea-worthy ships.

On the other hand the Gaels could offer culture and education to the Norse in return. They had also the Christian Faith which, in spite of bitter opposition from the Norse "Old Guard", was never in serious danger and gradually regained the upper hand.

All that was needed to bring the two nations together permanently was a catalyst and, as was discovered during the last war, the best way to bring people together is to subject them to a common misfortune and danger. Where a common enemy is involved, the most unlikely friendships will be formed and, for the Isles, the catalyst was that Magnus Berfott mentioned above (by the way, not Magnus Barelegs as most standard works call him). This King of Norway could not get it into his head that people who have been tortured, bereaved, seen their homes go up in flames and shivered on the moors are not the least bit likely to submit tamely to the man who has heaped these miseries upon them. The one thing Magnus accomplished during his short life was the forging of a lasting bond between native Scots and Norse settlers.

The effects of all this easing of tension can be seen in Islay in the large numbers of Norse names on the borders of the areas of primary settlement. Names which, although Norse in language, are quite different in character from the earlier groups.

In one way the Hebridean Norseman was at a disadvantage. The Isles were still predominantly Gaelic-speaking and he, once he had settled down, might well spend the rest of his life without once hearing from home or meeting anyone to talk to him in his mother tongue other than the other members of the small local Norse community. It is under such circumstances that local dialects develop and we can still see traces of this late Islay–Norse dialect in the new group of names.

The outstanding characteristic of this latest group is its use of the word "bólstaðr" for a farm of any sort, good or bad, large or small. In the whole of Norway this word occurs fewer than ninety times and in more than half these instances it has "mikil" (great) as its descriptive element, while in most of the others it has "helgi" (holy). Olsen[20] tells us that the word was in use for a farm about the beginning of the Viking era, that is, about the time that the settlers first came to Islay from Norway. In Norway itself the name never became very popular and died out after its first brief flicker but in Islay, where the Norse vocabulary must have tended to become progressively smaller as the language gradually decayed, it obviously became the only word in common use for a farm.

These later "bólstaðr" names rarely, if ever, appear with an adjective and in only two or three cases with a personal name: the rule is that they are governed by a noun in the genitive case and usually that noun is descriptive of the terrain. Thus we find that the richest of the Oa "bólstaðr", is Cornabus—Korna bolstaðr—Grain-store farm while on the low ground on the isthmus of the Rhinns we find Lyrabus—Leira bólstaðr—Mud-flat farm.

The word "bólstaðr" will do more for us than merely prove the existence of a local dialect of Norse.

In Norway the "bólstaðr" names are very local in character; they are native to the area from Agder northwards and hardly occur at all outside the two counties of Sogn ok Fjordane, which has twenty-one and Möre, which has twenty-seven. We may then conclude that our Norse ancestors in Islay came mainly from these districts. As the colonists were leaving there at the very time when, according to Olsen, the "bólstaðr" was coming into its own, it is hardly surprising that it should live on robustly among the emigrants long after it had been discarded at home. On the other hand we have no Helgibus or Mikilbus; only Nerebus in the Rhinns—the early area of settlement—may be said to conform to the ordinary Norse pattern and this, of course, is what we would expect if these names had been given by a generation which had never known Norway.

As has been said, these "bólstaðr" names which we discuss now, occur outside the areas of early settlement. They were given at a time when Gael and Norse had become sufficiently reconciled to make the need for national boundaries a thing of the past. Nevertheless, it is very noticeable that out of the large number of Norse names found between Uisge an t-Suidhe and Port Askaig only one Norse name definitely associated with this particular late expansion is found on the east of the present A846. In other words, friendship for the Norse did not extend to letting them get into a position where they could cut the valuable Scotland–Ireland trade-route running from Lough Foyle—Lochindaal—Port Askaig—Jura—Knapdale.

These later "bólstaðr" names form:—

(1) A triangular block between Loch Gruineirt, Lochindaal and Bridgend, with a healthy off-shoot up the west side of the strath to the Sound of Islay.
(2) A semi-circle around the eastern marches of the old Oa settlement.

Other than Grobolls, there are no names of this sort associated with the smaller Garloist settlement so we may assume that this settlement was a failure.

There are two names, both of vanished farms, which may conceivably contain the names of Gall-Gàidheil: (Cnocan) Bhrannabuis (gen.) and (Dun) Chollapus. The lenition of these descriptive elements shows that they were understood to contain Masculine names (cf. MacDhòmhnaill, MacDhughaill, Dùn Phàrlain—MacDonald, MacDougall, Dunfermline). Brannabus (Oa settlement) could be Brian's bólstaðr influenced by Norse pronounciation and Collapus (Kilmeny) either G. Colla or N. Kolle.

By the time these names were being given, Norse language in the Isles had had its day. No doubt it remained for many years the language of the fireside but family-trees such as that of Somerled show that Gaelic personal names were replacing Norse and no doubt Gaelic had become once again the language of business. As early as 1408 the Norse names of the Oa had taken on their modern form[21] although this, on account of its isolated position, is precisely that area in which one would assume that Norse held on longest as a spoken language.

Here are the "bólstaðr" names:—

(a) Oa Settlement:—

Asabus[22] Àsar bólstaðr   Farm of the Ridge.

Brannabus   (?) Brian's Farm.

Coillabus   Kelda Bólstaðr   Boggy Farm.

Cornabus   Korna Bólstaðr   Corn-store Farm.

Cracabus   Kraka Bólstaðr   (?) If Norse, Farm of the Poles? Standing Stones but, in view of its position beside the most impressive burial-mound on the island, might it not be a borrowing from G. "Creag"?

Kinnabus   Kinnar Bólstaðr   Hillside (lit. cheek) Farm.

Risabus   Hríss Bólstaðr   Brushwood Farm.

Tosabus   Húsa Bólstaðr   Farmsteading (near Baile Bhiocaire).

(b) Bridgend–Port Askaig Settlement:—

Carrabus   Kjarra Bólstaðr   Farm of the Thickets. Probably the scrub wood-land near Mid-Carrabus.

(Dùn) Chollapus   (?)   Doubtful, see text. There are no very obvious ruins near the dùn.

Coulabus   Kúla Bólstaðr   Round-hill Farm.

Eallabus   Hjalla Bólstaðr   Farm on the Ridge.

Eorrabus   (?) Eyrar Bólstaðr   Gravel-bank farm or possibly from a debased form of "hjord" = Cattle Farm.

Lyrabus   Leira Bólstaðr   Mud-flat Farm. Probably "leira" rather than "leir". At the time that would be an apt description. This land was drained and the river re-routed to flow into Lochindaal early last century.

Persabus   Presta Bólstaðr ⎰ Priests' Farm and Cross Farm. These two can be
Corsapol   Kross Bólstaðr ⎱ taken together (if we assume that the -pol = ból-staðr, as it probably d°es), since these are both Christian names, i.e. given after 1000 A.D. almost certainly, and both showing metathesis. Now meta-thesis was a feature of the later Norn dialect of Shetland and presumably this is the same process at work here i.e. metathesis was a feature of "Scottish" Norse. One may assume that the Norse took half the land of the chapel (Cill' Chaluim Chille) to form Persabus Farm.

Much the same has happened at Corsapol where there is a little ruined chapel, but the cross has gone. Its existence is attested by the derelict farm of Crois Mhór (G) nearby (Great Cross). It is just possible that the "cross" in question is one of the two removed by the Argyll Campbells, the one to serve as mercat cross at Inveraray (popular tradition says this came from Iona but, for obvious reasons, Iona would tend to be thought of as the source of any cross) and the other as mercat cross for the Earl's fine new Burgh of Campbeltown. This latter cross certainly came from Islay where it was erected by one of the MacEachern vicars of Kilchoman. If this is the cross of Corsapol, the farm name must be very late indeed.

Scarrabus   Skarar Bólstaðr   Farm on the Edge/margin. But why? Does it refer to its position on the edge of the arable land or is it a reference to the rim of hills around?

Steinabus   (Staoinabus)   Stein Bólstaðr   Stone Farm. This farm presents difficulties. It is named on no map and is not remembered by any of the local folk. From such evidence as one can glean from its position on the rent-rolls, etc. it may be the Norse name of the farm now known as Balle-martin. Most of the "baile" names here are rather late, but this may be a case of an older, Gaelic name recovering its lost status.

Torrabus   þoris Bólstaðr   (?) Thori's Farm. The derivation "Bull Farm" is impossible.

In addition to these we have the following:—

Bolsa   Bólstaðr   Farm. It lies out on the barren moors beyond Kilenallan. Its very existence points to the fact that latterly a "bólstaðr" might be no more than a croft or smallholding. It is hard to say what contacts it had with the outside world since the obvious road to it is straddled by two or three old Gaelic settlements.

Keppols   (?)   Keppa Bólstaðr   Kempa Bólstaðr   It has been suggested that this is from the verb, "keppa" to strive or seek after, and hence the place where gatherings were held. On the other hand, close at hand is the spot where Godred Crovan challenged the dragon according to an old Islay story and Hero Farm is not impossible. Modern: Ceapasadh.

Robolls   (?)   The Gaelic is Ròbolsa and it is just possible that the descriptive element is "hraun" = rough ground + bólstaðr.

There is at least one "stadr" name, Skerrols = Karl's Farm with prothetic s-. This name appears as Kerosay circa 1600 and (?) Carrissay in 1614.

Some other surviving Norse names from this settlement are:—

(Baile) Ghillin   Gil-in   The Gullies.

Laoigean   Loek-in   The Brook.

Staoisha   Steins á   River of the Stone (There is a big stone in the river).

Other names: Duisker, Baile Hearraidh, Balole and Baluilve are discussed elsewhere while Aighean = hæðin = the hill.

The two Norse names on the east side of the strath are (Dùn) Ghuthaire (which belongs to the Cattadale-Barradale group) and Scanlasdal, which is probably of Gall-Gàidheal origin, Scanlan's Dale.

While it is easy to read too much into scanty evidence, it is odd that on the periphery of both the Gartloist and the Oa Settlements we find a sheiling name, Gaelic "àiridh", associated with a Norse personal name. Above Storakaig we find Airidh Ghutharaidh, apparently Godfrey's sheiling and undoubtedly connected with the dùn of the same name just over the watershed. Was this the sheiling where the builders of this magnificent fort grazed their cattle? Or is this the home of the last and poorest of the Norse colonists? Excavation on the dùn may help with the answer. At all events, traditionally this Godfrey was a Mac-

Neill and it is worth noting that the Islay MacNeills did claim to be of Norse descent. Though Godfrey seems to have gained a syllable!

Again, behind Port Ellen, lies Brahunisary which would appear to be G. "bràigh" with a Norse personal name + àiridh but I have no opinion to offer regarding this person. Locally it is believed that this name contains "seisreach" a team of six horses but, for various reasons, this is unsatisfactory. If, as I believe, this was the home of a Norseman, we may say that he had acquired a fine Gaelic vocabulary of which, no doubt, he was proud. Just as today this island is full of people bearing good Highland names who can point with pride to the fact that they cannot understand one word of the language of their forebears, so seven hundred years ago the Islay Norse forsook for ever their native culture, losing at one stroke their language and their identity.

Postscript to the Norse Period

While the Norse will always be remembered as pirates and plunderers, we should not forget that most Norsemen were not murderers or warriors, but men of peace, farmers and fishers. There are few Norse names to remind us of war, there are many which build up in our minds a picture of decent working folk trying to keep a respectable family together. The Norse were, basically, just "people".

When we stand at the door of the ruin called Laoigean, we can almost hear the Norse kiddie point to the stream beyond the little garden and say: "Loek-in". We can stand at Kilmeny Kirk and imagine the Norse ploughman plodding home along the "Norse" side of the strath opposite us to the place now called Keppolsmore but still remembered by the older folk as "Na Schaws"—(sjot, nom. pl. = dwelling place). We can think of the shepherd grazing his sheep along the raised beach south of Saligo on Campa—(kambr—a ridge of hill, in fact, the raised beach).

Here are a few more names of this sort:—

Doodal   Dy dalr = Boggy Dale.
Tundal   Hund dalr = Dog Dale.
Osamail   A puzzle, but not "River-mouth Dale" as has been suggested because (1) it is not near a river-mouth (though Henderson tells us it has "a lovely river with a few outlets" whatever that means) and (2) the o- is short and the -s- palatalised. It may just conceivably be some form of the intensive "oesi-" with "holmr" = a hill. i.e. the Prominent Hill, or the like, with reference to the steep crags behind Kilchoman Kirk.
Alsaig   Hals vík = Harbour on the slope—the land rises steeply behind it.
Sgioba (East End Port Charlotte)   it is Sgepa in 1804—Skip A = River of the Ships and if it be objected that the tiny burn here is hardly navigable water, it may be said (1) that the creeks here are still in use for small craft and (2) there were probably fair quantities of timber still available in the glen even as late as the Norse period.
Scouller   Kúlar = The Knolls, with prothetic s-.

Stremnish   Straum-nes = The Ness of the Current—a most apt name. The form of the name is deceptive and in several works it is wrongly derived from "stremya". The -e- is actually a recent development: Stromynis (1496), Stromness (18th Century), Stramnish (1801).

The end of the Norse period was marked by the breakdown and disappearance of the language and the gradual assimilation of the Nordic peoples but it meant that, as the older generation died off, we were left with a large number of place-names which had become unintelligible and had to be given a Gaelic dress (Just as today we see, for example, the beautiful old name Eilean a' Chùirn become the hideous Churn Island). This was not, of course, an overnight affair; very often the meaning of a name was remembered perfectly well long after the Norse language had ceased to be spoken. Thus, Dean Munro, in the 16th century was told the meaning of the Norse name Jura, although it is highly improbable that Norse had been spoken there during the previous two hundred years.

As early as 1385 the Norse name Texa had been given a Gaelic guise and had become Eilean Tecsa as it is today (Helan Hexa: Fordun) and it is fair to assume that by then Eikis Dalr had become Glen Egidale and Forsa had become Eas Forsa.—Waterfall River.

This period is marked by the emergence of the word "baile" which was tacked on indiscriminately to Norse words: Baile Olaf—Balole, Baile Ulfr (?) Baluilve, Gil-in (The Gullies) becomes Baile Ghillin and probably both Baile Charraich and Baile Chlavan are originally Norse in form. Notice, however, that the process seems to be confined almost entirely to one small area of Kilmeny Parish: A mot did not become Baile Amot nor did Grasdal become Baile Ghrasdail. It would seem that in the Kilmeny area there was an earlier breakdown of the Norse language, a period of bi-lingualism when people thought with equal ease in both media. Another pointer to such a period is the name Shuna Bheinn, where, of course, the normal Gaelic order of the words would be Beinn Shuna. Shuna is for N. Huna = Knob and it was surely a man who could think with ease in Norse who named it Knob Mountain instead of G. Mountain (of the) Knob.

We find also part translations, also belonging to the bilingual period:

Druim an Stuin   Ridge (G) of the Stone (N). The ridge lying to the south of the Carragh Bàn = Steins hryrgr.

Tobar a Lì   Well (G) of the Hillside (N) = Brynnr a hlíð.

Srath Bhata   Valley (G) of the Water (N) (were it G. Valley of the Stick (a) it wouldn't mean much and (b) bata would not be lenited).=Vatns dalr or the like. Probably the odd name Bataichean Bàna is also connected with this word.

Na Ballan (E. Orsay)   Bali-nn The (G) the Grassy Bank (N) again takes us to a generation which did not understand Norse. They did not know about the Norse Def. Article and assumed it to be the Gaelic plural.

Another possible name of this sort is Airidh/Coire Sgallaidh, where Sgallaidh (short a) may be skalli (N) a bald head, with reference to the bare summit of Cladville immediately above but can hardly be Skáli (N) a hut.

(Cnoc) Amanda   We are back with those speaking a corrupt, slangy Norse with Cnoc Amanda = Hill (G) of the Confluence (N. A mót).

Although not strictly Islay names, we have (1) Reis an t-Strutha and (2) Reis Mhic Phàidein, two islets in the Sound of Jura, where the Coire Bhreacain currents race by, sometimes in a quite terrifying manner. These are Norse "röst" = a sea-race, a strong current (1) Gaelic "sruth" of similar meaning (tautology) and (2) the genitive of MacFadyen, MacFadyen's sea-race, though who he was, we cannot say. Here is a case where the rising generation, not knowing the precise meaning of the word, but knowing that it belonged in the Sound of Jura, wrongly applied it to the islets.

Duisker may be Dysjar sker—Cairn rock. If so " sker " too changed its meaning from "sea rock" to just "rock". In Islay it came to be sgeir=(1) skerry, (2) peat bank.

---

[1] There may have been a raid as early as 786 on Portland.

[2] The Scottish/Irish colony in Iceland appears to have lain on the east side of the island under Snae Fell and on the Lagar Fljot where we find such names as Pap ey = Priest isle, Kirkjubol = Church farm, Egilsstadir = Church (Gaelic) + Farm.

[3] Elrifrica—various spellings.

[4] Daimhsgeir is usually taken to be Stag skerry, referring to the fact (possibly correct) that deer swim the Sound from Islay and land there but the correct Gaelic for this would be Sgeir nan Damh. Daimhsgeir, if Gaelic, would have to mean Skerry of a (single) stag, which hardly makes sense.

[5] -aig, -uig. Usually this element represents vík = bay/harbour as in Sannaig = Sand vík. Sometimes it is skik = strip of land as in Stora(h): kaig = Big strip, Uigeaskaig = Viga's strip. Sometimes, at least on the Continent, it represents the Latin vicus = town as in Slesvig = Slie town. It remains to be proved that this is the element in Fòrnisaig = (?) Forni's town.

[6] Brjost dalr = First line dale has been suggested here because there are parallel dales inland but that should yield "Briasdail".

[7] There is actually a Gaelic word "àros" = a dwelling and it has been suggested that the bay takes its name from the residence of the Kildalton clergy. The objection here is that the more natural thing to do would have been to call the bay after the *church* rather than after the residential quarters. Also, the word is decidedly rare in place-names. Usually it means "palace" or "abode".

[8] Only excavation will show if the Norse found it occupied.

[9] Krókr, which has been borrowed as a masculine noun is masculine in Norse too.

[10] The "Lowdown" Ferry to Ireland is mentioned in 1733.

[11] A possible case of "religious persecution" can be found in Gleann a Gaoidh (prob. for Gleann Mhic Aoidh), where there is a fairly substantial "cille" ruin and sanctuary wall for which no name survives. The Norse name for the glen survives as Dirgeadail, the name of the cemetery on the opposite side of the glen from the cille. The meaning is obscure to me. Dyrgju dalr would mean The Glen of the Dwarf Woman and this seems improbable. Just possibly it contains a corrupt rendering of the Gaelic saint's name.

[12] Tradition has it that the "king" of Conisby was Godred Crovan. There is no proof of this, but there is nothing inherently improbable about it.

[13] Bólstaðr became, first -bols, then -bus. In the case of this particular farm, both forms are in use. An old saying goes: Ceithir Busachan fichead ann an Ile. Twenty-four Busses in Islay. This is one of them! Again, Nerabols/bus contains a different descriptive element from Neriby (Kilarrow). Here it is "ner" as in "say", in the latter it is "ner" as in "get".

[14] Kúla (f) a knob, is a word which was fairly common for a round hill. It occurs here, again at Coul and Coulabus and, possibly, in Cultuinn.

[15] Kelsa—as in Callarnish (Lewis). There is a neolithic stone circle here and the Norse conceived of standing-stones as keels. In the Graenlendinga Saga, which contains material from our period, we are told how the Norse discovered a place they named Vinland and which can hardly be any place other than the New England coast. During their explorations, their ship ran ashore and damaged its keel so badly that they had to cut a new one. The damaged keel was set up on the headland and they named the place Kjalarness.

[16] Behind Tormisdale is the old farm of Fòrnisaig. This is a strange name. It cannot contain "vík" as it is well inland and there is no such word as "fórni" in Norse, as far as I can discover. Strangely, Fòrnisaig occurs in none of the lists earlier than last century but in 1494 there is reference to the lands of Torlissay. The location of this place is uncertain but it might, just possibly, be an older form of Fòrnisaig. This does not help much in finding what the name means though Torlussay does appear to be a "staðr" name.

Another difficult name is Ellister. By its appearance in English it should be either Cave smallholding (gen. hellis) or Holy smallholding (helgu) and both would be quite in the "spirit" of Norse names. The difficulty is that, firstly, the farm is not a smallholding: it is a double farm, split up very early because it was too large to manage, and also, the Gaelic name is actually Aolistadh. It is possibly "Ey-land staðr"—the lands included the big island off Portnahaven. On the other hand, it may, just possibly be a Gaelic name.

[17] This refers to an Islay "trick" of sticking on an s- at the beginning of a word, e.g. sadharcan for adharcan—a plover.

[18] Older Smaulli.

[19] Torra might be the old plural of "torr" a heap, a mound and this would appear to be borne out by the name "Druim nan Torran" nearby. On the other hand, Irish-type plurals such as this are uncommon and, in fact, the name would not be very suitable. Popular folk etymology could account for this "Druim".

n.b.—Batachan Bàna is probably Norse too but we will consider it later.

[20] Farms and Fanes of Ancient Norway.

[21] Title deed granted to Brian Mackay by Donald of Islay, May 1408.

[22] The Farm, now ruinous, lay to the south of the modern church. Port Asabuis on the East would point to the existence of a recognised Norse right of way through the Gaels' lands.

CHAPTER 8

NA BAILTEAN

The Land Measures

When we today ask how big a farm or garden is, we expect the answer to be so many acres or hectares—i.e. we expect to be told the extent of the surface area. Such an idea would never have crossed the minds of the earliest farmers in Islay as there was no known way of measuring the extent of a farm. Indeed, any such measure would have been of purely academic interest since they were concerned, not with the area, but with the amount of produce which could be expected annually. It was on the produce figures that farms were valued. Thus Proaig, which is a farm of vast extent, a sizeable part of the entire island, was reckoned a small farm while Esknish, a fraction of its size, was reckoned as twice Proaig. This must be borne in mind for an understanding of what follows.

When the early settlers from Ireland seized the land, driving the older inhabitants into the hills, they settled in compact "bailtean" or townships. We can get some idea of what these looked like from a visit to Lewis, where some of these old-time townships still survive. (Baile, pl. bailtean = a township, as in Ballygrant = Store Town. The names and locations of these earliest townships have been dealt with above (Chapter 3).

In the fullness of time these "bailtean" became overcrowded and each was halved to give two half-towns or leth-bhailtean. New steadings were erected on virgin ground and, presto, two farms where one had been before! These half-towns were subsequently divided again and again until one had the following:—

Baile	1
leth-bhaile	$\frac{1}{2}$
ceathramh	$\frac{1}{4}$
ochdamh	$\frac{1}{8}$

ochdamh $\frac{1}{8}$ A sixteenth was called a leorthus (various spellings) apparently meaning the smallest farm that would keep a family. Tenants of smaller units needed supplementary income. Various names were given to the tiny units, cow-lands and the like.[1]

Rent was normally paid in kind—or only partly in cash.

With the introduction of a money-based economy a value had to be put on the old Celtic "baile" and it was agreed to reckon it as the equivalent of a

Lowland ten-markland (with the mark standing at 13/4d (66⅔p)), this gave it a valuation of £6 13/4d or £6 - 66⅔p).[2]

We can make up a rental table:—

baile	£6	13/4 = £6 - 66⅔p.
½ baile	£3	6/8 = £3 - 33⅓p.
¼ baile	£1	13/4 = £1 - 66⅔p.
⅛ baile	16/8 =	83⅓p. (a handy-sized farm)
1/16 baile	8/4 =	41⅔p. (one leorthus).[3]

National taxes were levied at a rate fixed annually by the Commissioners of Supply and were levied on each quarter-land i.e. the principal Scottish tax was a tax on land, not on income. This method of tax-collection survived in Islay at least until last century.[4]

Three of these ancient "division" names survive in Islay and, surprisingly, two are in the Rhinns, in the densest area of Norse settlement. This goes to show that Gael and Norse could and did live together. Here they are:—

Octomore = An t-Ochdamh Mór   the Big Eighth (see above).
Octofad = An t-Ochdamh Fada   the Long Eighth.
Octovullin = Ochdamh a' Mhuilinn   the Mill Eighth.
Traces survive of one or two others in the rent-rolls.[5]

Later "baile" came to be used for any settlement or town, hence such names as:—

Bailevony   Baile a' Mhonaidh   Township of the Moor.
Ballymeanach   Am Baile Meadhonach   The Township in the Midst.
Ballygrant   Baile Grana   Grain Town, Store Town—where the Lords of the Isles had their grange.

For some reason both Scotland and Ireland were slow to develop money economies. Even the savages who occupied South Britain after the Roman withdrawal had a highly developed system of coinage long before our own ancestors. The usual explanation given for this is that the pastoral side of farming was much more attractive to the Celt than mere crop-growing and so, in practice, cattle served as a sort of coin of the realm and it is true that even as late as the 15th century cattle were accepted as payment of feudal dues in the Highlands. It is, however, more than doubtful if this is the whole answer.

The first mention of an Irish coinage is a note in the Annals stating that in 1170—i.e. two years before the loss of Independence—money was coined at Clonmacnois. Scotland was only slightly earlier as we happen to know that David I (1124–1153) coined "sterling" pennies. The site of the old mint is still shown in Stirling Castle.

The Norse were actually the first in Ireland to use money and their money system was based on the ounce, a block of silver divided into twenty silver pennies[6], and the Norse, predictably, imposed their own system of rental on the occupied areas of Scotland. The Ounceland = Gaelic—Tìr Unga and anglicised "terung" appears to have been roughly equated to the "baile" and to have worked out at a tax of one penny on each house in the "baile". Hence we find Pennylands, and, having developed from them, Halfpennylands and Farthinglands. Mull and Kintyre have plenty of names of this sort; e.g. Pennygowan =

Peighinn a' Ghobhann = the Blacksmith's Pennyland but, for no very obvious reason, Islay has none! Several unconvincing explanations have been put forward but the most probable would appear to be that there was a fairly competent local administration on the island which simply continued to function under the Norse occupation. I should mention that there is one name in Islay containing "penny", Creag na Peighinn, but although it is not known how it received its name, it is almost certainly not a valuation name as this has never been a farm. Much more likely it is the place where someone either lost, or found, a silver penny and the name "stuck".

Na Bailtean

Baile is a word of rather obscure origin. It appears originally to have meant "a place" and so, "a district". From that it becomes "a particular place within the district" and eventually "a township". It has not travelled quite as far along the road as the Teutonic parallel "heim" which, from being an utterly impersonal word meaning "world", comes to be one of the friendliest of all words, "home". Here, however, is proof that humans, wherever they may be, think along very similar lines.

For our purposes, "baile" means a township, a cluster of buildings housing one or more families and forming a viable unit. Early Irish custom invested the word with a legal significance. It is used in this way in "baile-biadhtaigh" = a thirtieth of an Irish barony, and in "baile-fearainn" = a farm, and it is in this latter sense that we meet it.

We saw that the original Islay settlements or "bailtean" were divided into halves (leth-bhailtean), quarters (ceathraimh), and so on but the word "baile" itself seems to be of rare occurrence in these early place-names. (A parallel might be found in the everyday English word "city" which occurs only in Mexico City, Guatemala City, Panama City and a very few others). Most of these dozens of "Bal-" and "Bally-" names with which the maps of Scotland and Ireland are peppered are relatively late—most, though, of course, not all: Halftown (Leth-Bhaile) near Inveraray probably goes back to the earliest days of Gaelic settlement in the area but Balole and Baluilve Olaf's Baile and Ulfr's Baile are obviously late. At earliest they belong to the last days of spoken Norse in the Isles (cf. p. 88). That is, they belong to the 12th–13th centuries when Norse was dying but Norse personal names had not yet received their modern Gaelic dress. Notice too that by this time the word "baile" has taken on a different shade of meaning. To the early settlers it meant "farm" in the sense of a definite unit worth so much in rental, now it just means a piece of land with a farmhouse.

Proof of the lateness of "baile" names is readily available. The Isle of Man has an interesting name Ballakilpheric where "baile" is superimposed upon an earlier church name and this is most unlikely to have taken place until after the memory of the old Irish Church had died out and few people knew what "cille" meant. Again, such names as Balgown (Wigton), Balmae (Kirkcudbright) and Balmore (Stirlingshire), all in former Strathclyde, cannot be much earlier than the last days of Welsh speech in the area and obviously must date from after the end of Cymrian independence in 1018. "Obviously", because these baile names are scattered, not clustered together as they would have been had they been the result of invasion and settlement in hostile territory. As if to drive home this point of lateness, we find "Balmaclellan" in Kirkcudbright. "Maclellan" is "Son of Gille Fhaolain", not the saint of St. Fillans but the saint of the same name who is found on the West Coast—Kilellan, Islay; Renfrew, Lochalsh, etc. Now although the saint in question died in the early centuries of Christianity, the followers lived on for generations in the original settlements, taking the title "Maoil" = Tonsured Ones of the saint (singular "maol"). Not till after the rise of Roman Catholicism in the early eleventh century did the now more or less discredited followers of the Old Order discard their tonsure and take the less controversial title "gille" = servant.

There is a fair number of names, mainly in the South–Central Highland area, where we find "baile" with a personal, and usually a saint's name. These may, of course, be cases where some long-deceased farmer had the same name as a saint but it is possible that in some cases at least we are dealing with sites where "cille" has been replaced by the secular "baile". We might cite Balmaha (Stirlingshire) and Balmalcolm (Perthshire) as probable cases of such a change.

Another set of late "baile" names includes such places as Ballevicar = Baile Bhiocaire = The Vicar's Township where we are dealing with the clergy of the Roman Church but Islay's Ballinaby is a puzzle. It ought to be late but since there never was, at least as far as we know, an abbey of the Roman type established at Kilchoman, this must be, surely, a "baile" belonging to the abbots of the Irish Church. I certainly have never heard of any tradition linking the lands with Iona, Oronsay or any other Mediaeval abbey. Again the Gaelic is Bail'an Àba and this long a- would suggest a borrowing direct from the Hebrew rather than from Latin.

While most of these names mentioned above can be dated with reasonable certainty, it is worth noting that many pitfalls await the unwary. I personally, had always believed that Balallan (Lewis) = Pretty Village was the work of some romantic Victorian. I find, on investigation, that the name has actually a quite respectable pedigree behind it. In investigating any field of human activity one must budget for the unexpected!

Of all the unexpected names, however, our worst puzzle is undoubtedly Baile Chatrigan (Oa). At first sight this is just a Masculine proper noun in the Genitive -an ordinary O stem. Second glances reveal some difficulties. Firstly its vowels are impossible for a modern Gaelic word and further, one would have expected the inter-vocalic -g- to be lenited. Here we are dealing with a name of very great antiquity. In all probability there is a tribal name sewn up inside this modern-looking word. Catrigan might well be Old Celtic "Queen of Battle" (made masculine by analogy) and such a "queen" would be tutulary goddess of a tribe called the Catriges. Is it possible that it is this tribe and not wild cats that are commemorated in Creag a' Chait, Cattadale, and so on?

Another interesting "baile" is Ballemartin (Baile Mhàrtuin) = Martin's town. This name does not occur in the lists until the eighteenth century when it appears to replace the Norse "Steinabus" (various spellings) = Stone Steading

94

—obviously referring to the traces of Primitive Man in the area. The question is, was Baile Mhàrtuin a pre-Norse name, in which case the little burial-ground close to the steading is a dedication to St. Martin, or is Martin simply the name of a seventeenth-century farmer with aspirations to immortality? We shall never know for sure but some Gaelic names did survive alongside the Norse and eventually regained their former importance as the Norse died out. One example is N. Ilar Sund which became Caol Ile again after the end of Norse rule. As for "Steinabus" nobody remembers this name at all.

Farming

It seems that no one has ever had the courage to write a complete account of the complicated, indeed weird and wonderful system of land tenure and farming which obtained in the Highlands until last century and this is certainly not it! The slogan "Cut out the middle man" had no place in Highland thinking, and "middle men" of all sorts abounded.

At the top of the tree was the "laird" or "tighearna" who held his land either direct from the Crown or from some more important landowner than himself. He either let the land direct to tenant farmers or to a sort of "gentleman farmer" called a tacksman who would himself let some of the land. Under these again were the cottars, holding their land in return for labour. Farms were not usually let to a single individual. Rather a farmer would have a share in a farm according to his wealth. For example, in 1614 or thereabouts Baile Chatrigan was in the hands of one Alex. Campbell, who is described as "bailiff", i.e. a fairly substantial individual. By about 1680 the Campbell family had gone and we find as tenants: Archd. Hunter, Gillechalum (Malcolm) McCaldret (sic), Donald McKisag (MacIsaac), William Dollas (Dallas) and Hugh Dollas. Half a century later this quarterland has been divided into thirty-two parts held as follows:— Archd. and Alex. Graham, eight parts; Alex. McNabb, four parts; Duncan McDugald, four parts; Donald Calder, four parts; Kate Sutherland, four parts; Andrew McGibbon and Margaret McIlbryde (MacBride), four parts, and John McGilchrist, four parts. Another eight years sees great changes. Now the tenants are:—Duncan McDougall, William and Thomas Calder, Duncan and Hector McGibbon, John Calder and John McGilchrist. (This last is taken from the Rental of 1741, the twilight period before Culloden). In addition, of course, there were the cottars, unnamed on the Rent Roll.

There were various hangers-on, all "part of the system" who appeared at intervals, the most important being the miller, who appeared as if by magic every harvest-time. Farms were often, if not usually, "thirled" to a mill, and the miller had the right to compel all farmers in his area to bring their corn to him for threshing. Illicit milling was frowned upon almost as illicit distilling is today. Incidentally, leases were usually for nineteen years, each of the tenants having his share of the arable in accordance with the rent paid and the right to run cattle on the common grazing.

Beggars were frowned on and were indeed, liable to severe penalties. So keen were people to avoid the stigma attached to the name that respectable

95

folk often preferred to go hungry rather than seek charity. But, on the other hand, there was a sort of "honourable" begging described in Braid Scots as "thigging" and in Gaelic as "faoighe". The thigger, who might be a young man wanting to marry, or a man whose cattle had been lost, or something of the sort, simply went from friend to friend and from neighbour to neighbour making his wants known and, apparently, it was considered most unlucky to send away an honest thigger empty-handed. However, an old proverb tells us: Cha n-e rogha nam muc a gheibh fear na faoighe—the thigger doesn't get the pick of the pigs!

The advantages of this rather complicated social organisation are not, at first, obvious. They existed nevertheless and there were many to bewail the passing of the old order, the more so as it was replaced all too often by the rapacious, bullying landlordism of the 19th century which is not quite dead even today. The great merit of the old system was that people mattered. A learned Scot of the early nineteenth century remarked that, in his grandfather's time, if you wanted to know how wealthy a man was, you asked how many men he had; in his father's time you asked how many cattle he had and now, in his own time, you asked how much money he had. And, indeed, this does sum things up exactly. Under the old system everybody had his place in the scheme of things, everybody fitted into the general pattern. Laird and tacksman depended on the farmers, farmers depended on the cottars and, in time of want, the tenants depended on the laird[7]. Again, since it was in the laird's own interest to have a happy, contented peasantry, he was perfectly willing to finance promising young lads, granting them long-term loans interest-free (or almost so) to set them up in farms (this was known as steilbow tenure).

The old system could not have survived for ever, but Culloden Moor hastened the end in a brutal and demoralising manner, the effects of which are still painfully obvious throughout the Highlands and Islands. The old lairds, ruined by events outwith their control, often sold out to shoddy businessmen (as happened in Sutherland) who "cleared" the land and ran cattle on it. Most of the older gentry who hung on appear to have adopted the "if you can't beat them, join them" philosophy and became just as cruel and mean-spirited as their neighbours from the South. Times had changed; the old order had gone but it is indeed hard to understand how to justify the action of man who threw sixty of his tenants (roughly three hundred people) out onto the hillside so that their houses could be destroyed and then had the temerity to take those who protested to court! This happened at Sollas, North Uist in 1849 and was one case among hundreds from that period. In fact, the story of the Highland Clearances must make everyone who studies it come to the conclusion that contempt and disgust are all that the Highland "aristocrat" deserves. It is easy to forget that there are two sides to every story and that there were good landlords too.

For political reasons, the national Church comes badly out of it. One of the first acts of the United Kingdom Parliament forced the English system of lay patronage upon Scotland (in defiance of the conditions of the Act of Union be it said). It is said that this system works very well in England but, in Scotland, it produced a type of sycophantic parson who typified all that was foul in smug self-righteousness and who remembered always the debt he owed to "His

Lordship". As far as I know, only one Highland minister (the Rev. Donald Sage) had the courage to stand up and damn these evil people and their henchmen but, in fairness, when once a lead was given, most of these ministers did rise up and leave the Establishment, often enduring great hardship for themselves and their families. (See the contemporary remarks of Lord Cockburn on the Disruption or any good text-book on the subject.)

Islay and the adjacent areas escaped the worst of things. The Shawfield Campbells who owned the island at the time were, in fact, good, enlightened and cultured folk and we today are still reaping the rewards for the time and money expended on the island by them. Jura was perhaps less fortunate. The Rev. Alex. Kennedy of Jura, writing in 1844 of local conditions (Stat. Acc. of Scotland, Jura Parish) says, inter alia; "Mr. Campbell of Jura . . . acted in the most liberal and exemplary manner . . .", and ". . . the liberality of the principal heritor, Mr. Campbell of Jura . . ." In point of fact it is hard, even to-day, to find someone who has a good word to say for the actions of this family when at the height of its power.[8]

At present Islay is owned mainly by the Morrisons, who use the island as a holiday home and whose factor has expressed himself in public as wishing to see the smaller tenants " in an urban situation". The Ramsay family, who formerly owned most of the remainder have lost their lands. In fairness, they showed a great understanding for the islanders. Even John Ramsay's so-called Clearances which in the event, did leave the Oa derelict, seemed, at the time, to be giving a new start to people who were, by any standards, living in grossly unsatisfactory conditions. His well-meant actions have earned poor Ramsay much opprobrium but what he failed to understand was that the "Clearance" process, once started, was irreversible.

It would be idle to assert that West Highland agriculture was, in any sense, a fashion setter. Although Scottish agriculture in general seems to have set fairly high standards, much higher than is generally supposed, in some parts of the country methods had changed little since the late Iron Age. Most text-books (and all English authorities) are agreed that Scotland was backward. Some parts certainly were, but the following taken from the biography of Elizabeth Grant of Rothiemurchus [Memoirs of a Highland Lady (John Murray, London, 1960)], presents a picture rather at odds with that given in the standard works on the subject which unite in pointing out that modern agricultural method, like every other blessing, came to Scotland from south of the Border:—

page 50 (1807)

"My father turned the remainder of his time in the Highlands to farming account, for he was exceedingly interested in agriculture, particularly anxious to open the eyes of the Hertfordshire people, who at that time pursued the most miserable of the old-fashioned English systems. The first year we went to Twyford he had established a Scotch grieve there; he built a proper set of offices, introduced rotation crops, deep ploughing, weeding, hay made in three days, corn cut with a scythe, and housed as cut, cattle stall-fed; and I remember above all a field of turnips that all, far and near, came to look and wonder at— turnips in drills, and two feet apart in the rows, each turnip the size of a man's

G

97

head. It was the first such field seen in those parts, and so much admired by two-footed animals that little was left for the four-footed. All the lanes in the neighbourhood were strewn with the green tops cut off by the depredators. The Scotch farming made the Hertfordshire bumpkins stare . . ."

While this makes it quite clear that there was much good in Scottish agriculture, too much should not be read into it. Rather we should think of progressive and backward parts and, by and large and with notable exceptions, Argyll, on the eve of Culloden, appears to have had much in common with Hertfordshire. Land was still divided into in-field and out-field, the latter being used for grazing the cattle, under the charge of a herd-boy, while the former which was, of course, unfenced, was divided among the various tenants of the farm in accordance with their family requirements. When the soil of the in-field became impoverished through poor manuring, the tenants simply betook themselves to a fresh piece of land.

That actual cultivation was carried on in narrow strips or "rigs" (cf. Burns' mention of corn rigs), each family would have strips in different parts of the in-field. Ploughing was either by the old wood and iron plough, often owned in common, or by that extraordinary implement peculiar, as far as I know, to Western Scotland, the cas-chrom, or crooked-leg. It consisted of a leg-shaped piece of wood, the upper "leg" forming the handle and the "foot" being fitted with a metal toe-cap; on the side of the "ankle" was a stout wood or metal peg. The operator pushed the metal "toe" into the ground, downwards and forwards putting his foot against the peg to get the necessary pressure. When it had been driven far enough in, the handle was thrown to the side and the broad side of the "foot" turned the ground over. It is said that with a little practice, it became quicker to dig with the "cas-chrom" than with a modern spade and, indeed, it was still in use within living memory in the Long Island. Islay had also a special pattern, really a sort of digging-stick or dibble, called the "ceapa" which was used in the Rhinns until about 1940. Reaping was usually carried out by scythe but the small sickle continued in use on poorer farms probably until the late 18th century.

To make the rig system still more complicated, it was quite the accepted thing that all tenants exchanged rigs annually in order to ensure that everyone got a fair share of the good land. In practice, this meant that it was nobody's business to keep the rigs and the side ditches free from weeds—you could just leave that job to next year's occupant! If one goes hunting for rigs, the best place to look is on the hillside, rather than on what we today would consider the best land. This was to allow for drainage among a people who knew nothing of water-tables and how to regulate them.

As in the rest of Scotland, Islay's crops were oats (for food), barley (bere) for brewing and a good deal of flax for spinning. ("King Cotton" was eventually to ruin the Scottish linen trade and, in spite of many efforts to keep the linen industry alive—Keills village was built by the laird for weavers—no flax has been grown here for many years). During the eighteenth century occurred perhaps the biggest change ever in eating habits with the introduction of the potato. The potato was established in Islay by 1722.

During high summer when the crops were growing and in need of little attention, it was often possible to conserve the grazing around the steading by taking the cattle off to the higher moorland. On many farms it was the custom for the family to pack up and go off for a sort of holiday among the hills and a little sheiling-bothy called an "àirigh" was kept for the purpose.

There are many Gaelic poems which speak nostalgically of the "àirigh" and a surprising number of these "àirighean" have survived in place-name form.

Many preserve the name of the owner:—

Àirigh Ghutharaidh   Godred's Sheiling
Àirigh Mhic Dhòmhnaill   Said to have belonged to the Lords of the Isles.
Àirigh Mhaol Chaluim   Malcolm's Sheiling.
Loch Àirigh Dhaibhidh   The Loch of David's Sheiling.
   Some tell us about the nature of the place:—
Àirigh nan Clach   Sheiling of the Stones.
Àirigh nan Sithean   Sheiling of the Little (fairy) Hills as it stands but other
   explanations are possible (e.g. from venison).
Conas-àirigh   Gorse Sheiling.
Druim na h-Àirigh   Sheiling ridge.
Cloch-àirigh   Stoney Sheiling (preserving an ancient form of the modern
   "clach").[9]

A memory of the great days of the Lordship is preserved on the hill above their Capital at Finlaggan:—
Àirigh nan Caisteal   Sheiling of the Castles (but why is it plural?).

In these times it was necessary to bring the cattle in at night to a "crò" or "buaile". Both mean a cattle-fold—the celebrated Deirdre described Glen Etive as a "buaile-gréine", a cattlefold of the sun, but the latter carries also the idea of a place where the milking is done—at least in Islay. We find Cnoc na Buaile = cattle-fold hill in the Rhinns—the crò is, of course the word we have in Glen Croe, Mid Argyll.

A sheep-pen is a "fang"—Braid Scots "fank" and this we have in Rudha na Fainge—Sheep-pen Promontory (this is not the word in Fangdu).

SOME OTHER FARM NAMES.

As Gaelic, unlike Norse, has been spoken continuously in Islay since the fifth century at least, it is very hard to "date" any simple descriptive name. For example, Kintra (Kildalton)—"Cionn Tràghad"—End of the Strand in Dative-Locative form occurs in a list dated to 1408 so we know that it is at least that age and, further, from its rather antique form, we may conjecture that it is actually a good deal older. Unfortunately there are a great many names where even that degree of probability is impossible. What of Bun an Uillt = Mouth of the Stream? Or Cnoc Donn = Brown Hill? There is absolutely no way of telling whether these names are one hundred or one thousand years old.

One name which can generally be taken to be old is "gart" (gort) = a field, especially a field of oats. It is also, oddly enough, the Gaelic name for the letter G. In Ireland this word appears in Gort an Cháirn (Gortacorn) which is the same as Gartocharn (Dunbarton). In Scotland it is associated with the period of Gaelic expansion into the Lowlands—roughly 11th–12th centuries: Perthshire has Gart, near Callander, Lanarkshire has Gartcosh (probably a personal name). Gartferry = Gart Foraidh, Field of the Mound; Glasgow has Gartnavel—Possibly Orchard and Dunbartonshire has Gartocharn = Cairn Field.

The pattern in Islay is rather odd. We have a group of five which were probably originally adjacent on the East of Lochindaal (there are intrusive Norse farms between them now):—

Gart a' Chosain   doubtful. ? Foot-path Field.

Gart Loisgt   Burnt Field.

Gart Meadhoin   Mid Field (obviously).

Gart na Tràghad   Shore Field.

Gart Breac   Speckled Field.

Kilmeny Parish has three, of which one is lost but which certainly lay near Gartness.

Gartness   Gart an Easa   Waterfall Field.

Gart an Tiobairt   Field of the Well (lost)—Tiobrad is an ancient word for a well.[10]

Seanghart   Old (i.e. long cultivated) Field.

I have found none in Kildalton and Oa, and none in Kilchiaran Parish.

Kilchoman has:—

Gart a' Charraigh   Standing-stone field—the stone is beside the steading.

Gart an Lacha   Wild-duck Field (abandoned last century. The last tenants were, it is said, Robertsons, who had a "changeling" child).

If these last two names are ancient, it means that both lay within a stone's-throw of important Norse townships, Conisby and Bolsa. This suggests that, as has been said above, peace rather than war was the established way of things even where the immigrants were strongest.

The diminutive of "gart" is "gartan"—a little field, which is found in such names as Ardgartan, but is missing in Islay. Instead, Islay keeps a more ancient form of the diminutive—"goirtean". St. Columba himself is said to have been born at Goirtean, Co. Donegal.

"Goirtean" is as common as "gart" in Islay, though it is still missing in the Oa and in Kilchiaran Parish or, at least, I have found no trace of it in these places.

Kilarrow has:—

Goirtean Bhogaidh   Field of the boggy place.

Goirtean Tigh Ghille Mhuire (Gortanilivorrie). As Gilmour is a type of surname which can be dated with certainty to post 1000 A.D. this name must obviously be later still.

Kildalton has:—

Goirtean Dubh   Black/dark field.

Kilchoman has:—

Goirtean   Field and Goirtean nan Caorunn   Field of the Rowans.

Kilmeny has:—

Goirtean an Uruisg   Field of the sprite. If, as some assert, uruisg is a borrowing from Norse, and certainly it is not found in Ireland, then this name can be no earlier than the latter part of the Norse period and is probably later.

Gortenendlas   Goirtean an . . .   This site is lost. It lay near Lossit.

In the West of the parish lie:—

Corra-ghoirtean   Field of the peak (?) heron.

Goirtean Taod   Field of cords, but why? We can compare this name with Tigh nan Teud—Harpstring House in Perthshire as this "teud" is the same word as "taod".

[1] The $\frac{1}{3}$ was also, though rarely, used, especially in Ireland e.g. Trinamullin = Trian a' Mhuilinn = the Mill Third cf. Octovullin in Islay.

[2] At least as far as we are concerned though this was not the only valuation in the "new" money values, e.g. one davach (baile) = four marklands in a charter of James IV to John Mackenzie of Kintail.

[3] The most usual smaller units were:—

$\frac{1}{32}$ = the Còta Bàn or Groatland = 4/2d.

$\frac{1}{64}$ = the Dà sgillinn or Twopennyland (not to be confused with the Norse Pennyland) = 2/1d.

During the 18th century the devaluation of the Scottish coinage was such that for practical purposes 4/2d. Scots was reckoned = 4d. English and 2/1d. Scots = 2d. English.

[4] In the North, no doubt under Pictish influence, the Baile becomes the Davach (Doch, in place-names) and in the North-East it becomes Pit (Pictish, peit).

[5] In a grant made sometime before 1225 by the Earl Alwin to Maldowen, Dean of Lennox, mention is made of the three lower quarters of the lands of Luss called Achadhtulech (Hillock Field) and the other quarter which lies on the West of Luss. i.e. Luss was a "baile".

Again in 1506 James IV granted to John McGilleon of Lochboye (Maclaine of Lochbuidhe) a "great eighth of Aridsernula and an (? the) eighth of Knoknaseolaman" in Jura.

[6] Eighteen pence in the North (for reasons into which we need not go) Those interested in the subject will find an excellent article by D. Mackerrell in the Proceedings of the Society of Antiquaries of Scotland 1944.

[7] In Islay the Shawfield Campbells were ruined by the potato blight of the 1840s as all tenants claimed help from their laird.

[8] While not a great believer in the utterances of the Highland prophets I must record that, in early childhood, I heard it said that the Campbells would, one day, lose Jura and that the last of the family would be a cripple who would leave the island unnoticed, his worldly goods being carried on one white horse. Strangely this did come to pass in the 1930s when Campbell of Jura was forced to sell to an Englishman called Riley-Smith. The baggage of Mr. Campbell was taken to Small Isles on a white horse belonging to the incoming tenant and he himself slipped aboard the boat unnoticed.

[9] In fact this may not be an "àirigh" at all but an ancient Locative = Stone Place or the like.

[10] An old Port a Beul runs:—

Chaidh na mairt gu Gart an Tiobairt,
Chaidh iad ann gun teagamh idir.

CHAPTER 9

HILLS, LOCHS, ANIMALS and PLANTS, COLOURS, GALL GAIDHEIL, LORDS OF THE ISLES

In the very nature of things the Highlanders were bound to have several words to describe "hill", these being things of which they had rather a number!

The first, as it were, basic word for a mountain is "sliabh" and we have it in "Sliabh Gaoil" near Tarbert (Loch Fyne) and Sliabh Bhrothain in Islay (probably an ancient divinity is commemorated here—(the word is Gen. Singular, Masculine). But although "sliabh" has kept its original meaning in Ireland, in Scotland we generally find it used for an upland plain or a hill-slope and the commoner word for a mountain is "beinn" (ben) which originally meant a horn (Deirdre uses it in that sense—at least it is used in that sense in the "Lay" ascribed to her, and Cruachan Beann = Cruachan of the Peaks, shows it used in the earlier sense). From being a horn or the peak of a mountain-top, it becomes any mountain mass—Beinn Nimheis = Ben Nevis is the best-known of all.

The highest mountain in Islay is Beinn Bhiocaire (the Vicar's Mountain) but, unfortunately, we have no way of telling who the vicar was.[1] One may assume that he was one of the clergy attached to Kildalton who enjoyed walking on the hill—there is a somewhat similar case near Dunoon. Next in height comes Beinn Bhàn (the Fair, White Mountain) and it does, in fact, glow in the sunshine, the upper slopes being quarzite and almost bare of vegetation. Among others we have Beinn na Cailliche (Old Woman's Mountain and in this sense, the "Old Woman" is the goddess. Beinn has sometimes been tacked onto Norse hill names (tautology): Beinn Sholum (Mountain of) Sheep Mountain. The older word "sliabh" occurs here and there: Sliabh Mór = Big Moor (Kilmeny) but Big Hill (Kilchoman).

Another and most descriptive word is "maol", a bald pate—originally a priest's tonsure and this is perhaps the next in importance. Most of the rounded hills of the Oa are of this class: Maol Buidhe (Yellow Hill), Maol nan Eun (Bird Hill) and so on. Although this word is normally masculine, it appears to be feminine in Maoile Mhór (Big Hill).

"Creag" is a rock, cf. Craigendoran = Creag an Dobhrain—(Otter Rock), and we find it in Creag Mhór (Big Rock) near Kilnave while next to it is Càrn Mór and "càrn" is just a cairn whether natural or artificial.

"Cruach", a great, rounded hill is rare in Islay.

"Druim" is a ridge, a "backbone" as in Drymen—Druimean (Little Ridge) (Stirlingshire) and there are plenty of them in Kildalton Parish: Druim na Croise (Cross Ridge) and Tigh an Droma (gen.) (House of the Ridge) to name but two.

"Sgor, Sgorr" is a steep, craggy hill and we find it in Sgorr nam Faoileann which, as it stands, means Seagull Hill.

"Torr" is a large, steep hill, a "heap" and it occurs in Torr a' Chreamha— (Wild garlic Hill).

But by far the most common sort of hill word is "cnoc" (pron. craw-hk) with its Diminutive "cnocan". Cnoc a' Chaoruinn (Rowan Hill). Cnoc Donn (Brown Hill), Cnoc na Croiche (Gallows Hill), Cnoc a' Chlaidheimh (Hill of the Sword). Sometimes, as will be noticed, the reason for the name is self-evident but at other times, such as the last-named, it refers to some long-forgotten event which seemed very important at the time.

The name An Sgarbh at Rudha a' Mhàil would seem to be a place where Gaelic and Norse have acted on one another. The name is fairly common for a rocky ledge in Ireland but it has passed out of use in Scotland and I know of no other example of it. Possibly the Norse "skör" (rim, edge, etc.) as in Skara Brae may have influenced it.

Lochs

Lochindaal or, better, Loch na Dàlach, takes its name from the farm Dàil, as does Coille na Dàlach (Forest of Dàil) close by. Dàil is a difficult word to translate here. Dwelly's dictionary gives: delay, procrastination; meeting, convention, congress; attempt; friendship, attachment; fortress, fastness; credit, trust; preparation; interval; intermediate space between the rafters of a house, etc., etc. In fact, it would appear to mean almost anything! Probably the best meaning to give it here is "focal point", Dàil is the centre of the ancient settlement of Freag, the chief centre of the island, and the loch is the highway to it. We find much the same meaning in Jura for this word. The singularly incongruously sounding Lowlandman's Bay is for Dàil Ghall Focal point of the Foreigners. The "foreigners" in question being, not Lowlanders at all but Norsemen. This can be seen in the name of the farm at the head of the bay, Ardmeanish, which is the Gaelic "aird", a height, prefixed to Norse Megin-nes = principal ness. This is a fairly ordinary Norse way of naming an important natural feature and it tells us that, for the Norse, Lowlandman's Bay was more important than Small Isles.

Loch Gruineirt—Norse "Shallow fjord" with Gaelic "loch" has already been dealt with.

Loch Gorm, Gaelic: Blue Loch is an unusual type of name for a major feature and is probably fairly modern. My guess would be that it replaces a lost Norse name.

The names of few of the lesser lochs are of any great interest or even originality. Sometimes they take their name from the glen e.g. Loch Glenasdal, or from a nearby farm, e.g. Loch Kinnabus. Sometimes it is the shape e.g. Loch Fada (but not Loch Corr, which appears to be Loch Cobhair in Gaelic—the Frothy Loch). But sometimes loch names set fascinating problems. Who was the "Big Man" who gave his name to Loch an Fhir Mhóir, and what did he do thus to gain immortality? Whose "lads" are commemorated in Loch na Gillean and who is the Donald of Loch Dhòmhnaill? These are questions we can never hope to answer. Loch Clach a' Bhuaile is named after a stone marking a cattle-fold but the stone seems to have vanished. Loch nan Diol/Giol appears to be Leech Loch.[2]

More interesting is Loch Conailbhe. The cluster of small dùns with Gaelic names round Kilchiaran shows that the Bay was a centre of activity in the early days of Irish settlement and Loch Conailbhe lies in the midst of this area. The name is ancient but the meaning is hard to decide. According to structure it could contain the old word "ailbh", gen. = e, a flock but this does not explain the "con" which could be "dogs", which hardly makes sense or the intensive "con-" which would give us "Great Flock" which again hardly makes sense in an area of poor grazing land. Much more probable is that this loch preserves the name of an obscure deity, who was worshipped here. The presence of standing-stones in the area gives this weight because, although the Gaels certainly did not *erect* these standing-stones, there was no law preventing them from *using* an ancient religious site as, indeed, they did at Baile Neill.

Only a few more merit mention. The famous "tailless" trout of Loch nam Breac apparently have the tissues burned by the acidity of the water. It is true that the upland soil here has a very low pH. Loch Allan is an artificial loch developed for trout fishing. Loch Muchairt is odd. Firstly, there is no such word in Gaelic as "mucha(i)rt and attempts to tie it up with "luchairt" = a palace (referring to a presumed residence of Godred Crovan) fall down on the fact that there is no precedent for l- changing to m- after lenited -c known to me and also on the fact that "luchairt" comes from "longphort", lit. "harbour" and it is most unlikely that it would have taken the modern form. Can it be Irish "mú-chán", given as a heap of stone?

Loch an Nigheadaireachd apparently means the loch in which washing was done but one romantic story tells of the "bean-shidh", the harbinger of doom seen washing shrouds in this place. If the watcher be bold enough he can ask for whom the shroud is intended and possibly get inside information on the subject. Frankly, I doubt if it is worth the risks involved.

Animals and Plants

Our ancestors appear to have been very insensitive to their surroundings. The beauties of nature left them unmoved and when one comes on such names as Flowerdale, Lily Loch and the like, one can be quite sure that these are modern replacements of much more prosaic names. The famous Lily Loch at Dunoon is actually Loch nan Losgann—Frog Loch and, here in Islay, such

104

inanities as Beech Avenue, Antrim View, and the like, betoken a complete lack of understanding of the West Highlands.

Place-names in the Highlands occasionally mention animals. Here are some of those found locally:—

The buck   Rudha a' Bhuic   Buck Point. (sing.)

The bull   Boglach nan Tarbh   Bog of the Bulls.

The cat   Cattadale   Cat Dale; Creag a' Chait   Cat Rock. (sing.)

The cormorant   Sgeir nan Sgarbh   Skerry of the Cormorants.

The cow   Lorgba   Cow Land   (lorg is a strip of land here).

The deer   Dìollaid nam Fiadh   Saddle of the Deer; Druim nam Fiadh   Ridge of the Deer.

The wild duck   Gart an Lacha   Wild drake Field. (sing.)

The goose   Cnoc nan Geòidh   Hill of the Geese.

The goat   Eilean nan Gobhar   Goat Isle; Loch/Maol nan Gobhar—Goat Loch/hill.

The herring   Port nan Sgadan   Herring Bay.

The hind   Cnoc na h-Éilde   Hill of the Hind.

The horse   Druim nan Each   Ridge of the Horses.

The hound   Drochaid a' Mhadaidh   Hound Bridge. (sing.)[3]

The leech   Loch nan Giol   Leech Loch.

The mare   Lag nan Capull   Hollow of the Mares.

The pig   Eilean na Muice Duibhe   Isle of the Black Pig.

The seagull   Rudha na Faoileige   Seagull (sing.) Point.

The serpent   Cnoc na Nathrach   Serpent (sing.) Hill.

The sheep   Maol nan Caorach   Sheep Hill; also Loch nan Caorach.

The Stirk   Cnoc   a' Ghamhna Chaim   Hill of the half-blind Stirk.

The trout   Loch nam Breac   Trout Loch.

Plants are rarer:—

The Alder   Doire Fhearna   Alder Grove.

(?) The gorse   Carn Conas-àirigh   Hill of the Gorse Sheiling.

The hawthorn   Àird na Sgitheich   Hawthorn Height (Jura).

The ivy   Leac Éidhne   Flat Ivy-covered Rock.

The kale   Cnoc Càil   Kale Hill.

The oak   Doire Dharaich   Oak Grove.

The rowan   Cnoc a' Chaoruinn   Rowan-tree Hill.

Rushes   An t-Aonan Luachrach (aonach)   Rushy Moor.

The sloe   Loch Iarnan   Loch of the Sloes.

Tree   Cnoc na Craoibhe   Hill of the Tree.

Probably most of these names are relatively modern. Thus, in older language "craobh" meant a branch whereas here it obviously must have the modern meaning "tree".

Colour Names

Colour plays a greater part in our lives than most people realise. We can usually tell quite a lot about a person by his choice of clothes, wallpaper, and so on. Can we picture a Bardot in a parlour decorated in chocolate brown and bottle-green)? Or a Napoleon surrounded by pinks and flowery chintzes? Going further, we associate white with joy and black with grief and so white with purity, blessing and life, black with gloom, curse and death. These are the sort of associations we make in our minds as we look at the world around us. When we look at Beinn Bhàn, the fair Mountain, gleaming in the summer sunshine, its ancient quarzite reflecting the golden rays, we ask ourselves what other possible name it could have been given—and that although only a tiny part of the rock is actually exposed. Similarly Guala Dhubh, Black Mountain-side, the north-facing, cheerless and dangerous descent to Ardnahoe, could not have been given a better or more apt name. What too of Sgriob Ruadh—the Red Line, the fanciful name for the savage line of reddish cliffs below Mac-Arthur's Head. Could one have found a neater name? Ruadh means reddish or reddish-brown—not the colour of blood, which is "dearg"—and it carries with it the overtones of violence—Tuil ruadh, a violent flood (stronger: Ruadh thuil) ruadh-laith, cholera, and so on. More normally, however, a farmer applies the adjective "ruadh" to a field to do no more than denote the colour of the soil and the fact that, since the lighter colour reflects off the sun's rays in springtime, growth there can be expected to be sightly slower and later than on the darker soils. Normally the word for red is "dearg" and we find it applied to the harsh red cliffs of Beinn Dearg in Mid-Argyll. Dearg means danger, harsh reality, and where we see it on the map we should be on the look-out for risks!

Entirely different is "bàn", fair, white, blessed (the ordinary word for white is "geal" and it is rare in place-names as it is a rather "neutral" word, arousing no feelings of emotion). As we have seen, a happy thought on the part of our ancestors applied bàn to one of the most beautiful and comely of our mountains and a similar happy thought applied it to Jura as a kenning, an t-Eilean Bàn. Again it was a happy thought that applied it to the glorious golden strand of Kilchoman—Tràigh Bhàn.

Perhaps less obvious is "buidhe", yellow. Yellow is, however, a happy colour and although neither Carraig Bhuidhe—Yellow Rock nor Mullach Buidhe, Yellow Summit is particularly yellow in colouration, it is more than chance which sets them close to good harbours as prominent land-marks. As far as inland examples go, one invariably finds them in bright, cheerful spots.

"Liath" usually means hoary with age so when we see a Rudha Liath on the map we picture an old, lichened, grey crag jutting defiantly into the ocean and, as far as Islay's are concerned, we are not disappointed. As an actual colour "liath" means an *ugly* grey and it has this meaning in Tràigh Liath at Kildalton.

About "gorm" much might be said. Regularly it means blue- aodach gorm, blue cloth, flùr gorm, a blue flower, yet it also means green when referring to grass! It is, in fact, the colour of sky, sea and grass and when we find it in place-names, it usually denotes an intensity of colour which strikes the eye immediately: cf. Dùn Glas an Lòin Ghuirm (genitive) = the grey fort of the green meadow. Rarely, very rarely, "gorm" means black: duine gorm = negro and (poetic) caora ghorm = black-face sheep. Possibly this is the sense in Loch Gorm which, for most of the time is actually a rather dull colour. Notice here that Cairngorm in the Central Highlands shows yet another meaning for this versatile word: there it means great, outstanding, or even noble. Uaine, the ordinary word for green, is rare in place-names.

"Breac" is speckled or piebald—a' Bhratach Bhreac = the standard of the Knights Templars, but the verb formed from it also means to engrave or carve or cover with designs. It is tempting to look at Beinn Bhreac in the sunshine and pick out imaginary patterns on its face!

"Riabhach" means brindled or drab—usually a rather dull place in a place-name.

"Glas" normally means grey or pale, but it is also the colour of half-ripened corn and, rarely, of verdant grass—it is used in this sense in Psalm 23.

Just possibly this is the sense in Airigh Ghlas = ?Green sheiling but in Glas Eilean (weathered basalt) we see the usual meaning.

Fionn- (fionna-) has almost the same meaning as "bàn".

Odhar is dun, khaki-coloured or weather-beaten: Donn is brown, or unpromising of land.

Here is a selection of local examples illustrating the points made above:—

Bàn: Beinn Bhàn—Fair mountain.
           Carragh Bàn—White stone—burial-place of Godred Crovan.
           Lòn Bàn—Fair meadow.
           Tràigh Bhàn—Fair strand.
Breac: Beinn Bhreac—Speckled Mountain.
           Breac Achadh—Speckled field.
           Cnoc Breac—Speckled hill.
           Gart Breac—Speckled garden.
           but Loch nam Breac = Trout loch.
Buidhe: Blàr Buidhe—Yellow meadow.
           Carraig Bhuidhe—Yellow rock.
           Cleit Bhuidhe—Yellow reef (fr N. klettr).
           Druim Buidhe—Yellow ridge.
           Maoil Bhuidhe—Yellow bare hill (note gender O.S.).
           Mullach Buidhe—Yellow summit.
Dearg: Lag Dearg—Red dell
           Loch Dearg an Sgorra—Red loch of the steep hill.
Donn: Cnoc Donn—Brown hill.
           Uamhannan Donna—Brown caves.
Dubh: Carraig Dhubh—Black sea-rock.
           Cnoc Dubh—Black hill.
           Druim Dubh—Black ridge.
           Dubh-loch—Black lock.
           Eilean Dubh—Black isle.
           Gleann Dubh—Black glen.
           Guala Dhubh—Black hillside.
           Pàirc Dhubh—Black park/field.
           Pliadan Dubha—the Black plots of land.
           Sgarbh Dubh—Black rock.

	Sròn Dubh—Black point of land.
	Torr Dubh—Black hillock.
Fionn:	Fionna-phort—Fair haven.
Glas:	Airigh Ghlas—Grey (?green) sheiling.
	Glas eilean—Grey isle.
	Beinn Ghlas—Grey Mountain.
	Rudha Glas—Grey headland.
Gorm:	Dun Glas an Lòin Ghuirm—Grey fort of the green meadow.
	Loch Gorm—Blue (?dark) loch.
Liath:	Àirigh Liath—Grey sheiling.
	Cnoc Liath—Grey hill.
	Doire Liath—Grey grove.
	Mòine Liath—Grey moor.
	Tràigh Liath—Grey strand.
Odhar:	Coire Odhar—The dun corry.
	Lag Odhar—Dun hollow/dell.
Riabhach:	Gart Riabhach—Grey, brindled garden (i.e. covered with withered grass).
	Àird Ruadh—Red height.
Ruadh:	Ath Ruadh—Red ford.
	Bealach Ruadh—Red pass.
	Rudha Ruadh—Red promontory.
	Sgriob Ruadh—lit. Red line.
	Uillt Ruadha—Red streams.

The Gall-Gaidheil

To-day all too many of the young folk have to leave the island in search of work. This is, in fact, no new phenomenon, over centuries younger sons especially have found it impossible to make a living in Islay. To-day Glasgow is the magnet which attracts most of our young folk: throughout the Middle Ages Ireland was the magnet.

Ireland's history is a very sad one and it is impossible to give even the briefest account of Irish history without casting England in the rôle of the villain. Her misdeeds in Scotland pale into nothing compared with her behaviour in Ireland.

As we saw, the early historic period found Ireland struggling to develop a modern-style kingdom, but tending to lag behind the rest of Europe, politically, if in no other way. In the year 1172 a petty squabble between some of the kinglets led Diarmad, "King" of Leinster to flee to England to ask for help from Henry II. Henry gave help but, to cut a long story short, just as Edward I was to do in Scotland a century later, he himself claimed that, having given help, he was now overlord of the entire country. England refused to yield one inch on this claim to sovereignty until the 1920s and the final chapter in the sad saga which started so long ago is being written in the streets of Ulster to-day.

All through the Middle Ages mercenaries were in demand to fight the

Saxon tyrant and prominent among them were the young men from the West of Scotland, the Gall-Gàidheil or Foreign Youths (Anglised "Gallowglasses"). Even as late as the mid-seventeenth century Alasdair mac Colla (Alexander Macdonald of Colonsay) was killed in battle at Cnoc nan Dos in Southern Ireland.

There are many names in the North of Ireland which are very similar to names in Islay. This fact reminds us that the Clann Donald of Islay owned vast estates there and were, in fact, in the thick of the fight. It will be recalled that Iain Mór Tàinisdear of Dùn Naomhaig, at Lagavullin, second son of the Good John of Islay by his second wife, Margaret Stewart, Princess of Scotland, and brother of that Donald of Islay who brought the Isles to the zenith of their fortunes, married Marjory Bisset, daughter of John Bisset of the Glens of Antrim. Iain Mór inherited these estates and subsequently the family was to add more to its possessions.[4]

Here are some very familiar "Islay" names from East and Central Northern Ireland:—

Ballymoney = Baile Monaidh = Moor town—also in Rhinns near Portnahaven.
Ballymena = An Baile Meanach = Mid town—also in Rhinns near Portnahaven.
Ballygawley = Baile Ui Dhálaigh = O'Daly's town—Baile Ghàlaidh, Rinns.[5]
Martinstown = Baile Mhàrtuin—also in Kilmeny Parish.

We also have the river name An Lagan common to both places, but this is certainly a borrowing from a much, much earlier period, the period of the Earth Mother Cult when rivers were reckoned to be sacred.

No doubt in some cases of similar names, of which there are many more, it is pure coincidence, yet there are at least some among the above to remind us that Islay and Ireland were once very close friends and neighbours.

Tighearnan nan Eilean

It may seem to the reader that little has been said of the actual Lords of the Isles and how they ran their "kingdom". However, by their time the political map of Islay had assumed more-or-less its modern form, so their doings, though interesting, are hardly relevant.

Their principal residence was on Loch Finlaggan—Eilean a' Chaisteil (Castle Isle) while their Parliament met on the smaller adjacent isle, Eilean na Comhairle—Council Isle. A garrison was maintained on Loch Gorm, Caisteal Eilean Locha Ghuirm and another on Fraoch Eilean (Heather Isle) in the Sound of Islay. There was also a summer palace beside the present Kilchoman Church. Their principal harbour was at Tràigh an Luig—Strand of the Hollow just north of Goirtean while the elite corps of soldiery, the Luchd tighe, or Folk of the Household, had their barracks on the lochside just below the present Finlaggan Farm.

For purposes of local administration, the island was divided into three "wards", An Leargaidh (the Slope, the name that we have in Largs—Na Leargaidh Ghallda), which was the present Kildalton and Oa Parish; Na

Hearradh (the Heights, as in Harris), the central strath, and An Roinn (the Division), the present Rhinns. The first of these was sub-divided into the Oa, the central section or Leargaidh and An Lanndaidh (a name of doubtful meaning. In these days it was believed to be for Lann tigh a' mhanaich—the enclosure of the monk's house—apparently with reference to the religious settlement at Kildalton). This sub-division ran from Allt a' Chrochaire (Hangman's burn, Loch Knock) to, presumably, MacArthur's Head.

The Middleward too was sub-divided. Na Hearradh proper was only the present Kilmeny Parish but no special name appears to have survived for the present Kilarrow Parish. Apart from the "quoad sacra" division into two parishes, the Rhinns appears to have been administered as a single unit.

Some doubtful names

River Sorn: Sorn means a furnace in Gaelic and would be nonsensical applied here. We must therefore look elsewhere for a meaning.

There are several cases of the goddess Éire (gen. Éireann dat./loc. Éirinn) = Ireland being honoured in, or rather identified with rivers. Auldearn, for example, is just Allt Éireann (Ireland stream), the Earn is the Ireland (river), Findhorn is the Fair Ireland (river) and Deveron is its "twin", the Dark Ireland (river).

Now there is a pair of prefixes, so- and do- which date back to the days of the so-called dualistic religions when men conceived of, not one god, but two, the one representing the good and the other the bad and these two being equal in power. Ancient Persia was the home of this type of religion and there Mazda, God of Light was in perpetual combat with Ahriman, God of Darkness and, of course, this is the idea underlying the Findhorn and Deveron, the Whiteadder and Blackadder and so on though we to-day have lost so much of the old faith that we cannot clearly comprehend the thinking involved. We can, however, consider such words as soilleir and doilleir, clear and dull, sorcha and dorcha, bright and dark (as a proper noun, Sorcha translates the Latin name Clara), and so on. We also have the names Suibhne = Sweeny (cf. Castle Sween, MacSween and so on), and the name Duibhne = Dweeny, which is the original family name of the Campbells—Campbell means crooked mouth—a name given in pretended disparagement to protect a child from the fairies, who always tried to steal perfect infants.

With some diffidence I would suggest that Sorn stands for an original So-Éireann—Good Ireland (river). Its "twin" may be the river we call the Laggan. As it stands, Laggan seems to be the Calf (goddess river) and this name may well have been bestowed on it to avoid the use of an ill-omened name. (The ancients were very worried about such things. For example, Latin writers went to some pains to avoid ending a book, a poem, or even a sentence with a word of ill-omen and, when forced to use an "unlucky" word they uttered the words, "Omen absit!". This absolved them from possible evil consequences). It is just possible that an underlying, older name beginning with "do-" can account for such names as *Du*aich and Eilean na Muice *Du*ibhe nearby. This latter name, Isle of the Black Pig, which traditionally, as we saw above has Columban associations may also be a "religious" name in a pagan sense. It is significant that one of the ancient names for Ireland is Banba, and this means a piglet! Perhaps we should mention here that there are three principal names for Ireland: viz. Éire, Fotla and Banba. These are the names of three goddesses who ruled over the land and, as one might expect in a country colonised from Ireland, all these occur in Scotland. Athol is for Ath-Fotla = New Ireland, Éire is found in the river names (but not in Ayr—Gaelic, Inbhear Àir)[6] while, of course, it is Banba which we have in Banff.

Allallaidh : This appears to be a form of the word al—a cliff or rock—the name we have in Al Clut—Rock of Clyde, the Old British name for the place the Gaels called Dumbarton (Dùn Breatann—Fort of the Britons). Alaidh would mean Rock Place and this has apparently been reduplicated (Reduplication is a fairly common phenomenon in Scottish speech cf. Braid Scots: Come aff aff o' there! which a mother might shout to a child climbing up into danger, and the Gaelic: ann an leabhar—in a book, Lit. in in a book.

Mulindry : One can only remark that, had this name occurred in, say Ayrshire, there would be little doubt about its meaning and origin: it would be Welsh, Mill Village. One finds it hard to believe that there was a Welsh colony in Islay in ancient times. There is, however, just an outside chance that it is Welsh; Watson[7] found a name of similar type in Kintyre, Muchtre, which is the same as the Mochtre which occurs in Wales and means Swine Village and, of course, nearby Mulindry there is the enigmatic fort, Nòsbrig, which certainly looks as if it could be of British origin though it is much more likely to be Norse.

Almost certainly, however, the name does mean Mill Village but from different, though related forms of the same words (W. melin G. muileann W. tref and G. treabh—both these latter come from an Old Celtic word trebo—various endings depending on how it is used).[8] Here we might mention the name Mu*craidh* (Jura) which looks as if it is a name of the same type but is actually Swine Place, a fairly common type of name, cf. Cairnie (G. Càrnaigh, Place of Cairns; Rosemarkie (G. Ros Maircnidh), for Promontory of the Horse place (? horse brook) and many others. In Islay we have Tùrnachaidh near Kilchoman. This may be from G. tàirneach—thunder, and so, Place of Noise (of the sea).

111

[1] While, in all probability, this mountain preserves no more than the name of a long-departed vicar, a rather odd entry in the Irish Annals is worth mentioning:—

Tig. An. circa 625: Mongan, son of Fiachna Lurgan was struck with a stone by Arthur, Bicoir's son, a Briton, and perished and hence Bec Boirche said:—The wind blows cold over Islay; there are youths approaching in Kintyre: they will do a cruel deed thereby, they will slay Mongan son of Fiachna.

(This Mongan's father was king of the small Northern Irish semi-independent state of the Dal nAraide).

It is tempting to see in this entry a reference both to Beínn Bhiocaire and MacArthur's Head.

[2] Loch nan Giol (O.S.).

[3] Madadh-ruadh is a fox and the New Statistical Account of Scotland (Kildalton Parish) does inform us that the fox was once found in the parish but was, by then, extinct.

[4] The grandfather of this Iain Mór, that Aonghus Òg whose help at Bannockburn tipped the scales at the critical moment and gained Scotland's greatest military triumph, married the daughter of Connbuidh O'Cathan, Lord of Limavady in Ulster. This seems to have been the Clan Donald's first incursion into Irish affairs.

[5] Strangely these same "baile" names reappear in the Isle of Man. We find there also several "ceathramh" names, Kerrowmoar, Kerrowglass (cf. p. 91), some of the Norse names, e.g. Geaylin = (Baile) Gillin and Cooil = Cuil and the odd name Glascoe. cf. Glasgo Beag (Kilmeny) which is not the same as Glasgow (city).

[6] There is a mention in the Islay rentals of a farm called Heryne, which looks like Eirinn (locataive), but its much more likely to be for Aoireann, a mission station at which, in olden days, Mass would be said. The location of the place is unknown to me.

[7] History of the Celtic Place-names of Scotland (Blackwood).

[8] The word treabh is rare in Irish and Western Scottish names though not unknown. Perhaps the best-known example is Antrim—Aon treabh—Single (pre-eminent) dwelling (Aon—one is used in this sense in Angus—Aonghus—One Choice, Pre-eminent person).

GLOSSARY OF PLACE NAMES

This contains most (though not all) of the names mentioned in the text and is intended to give the reader some idea of the type of names to be found. Most of those given are straightforward but I include some more difficult and controversial names.

G.—Gaelic;   N.—Norse;   A.—Ancient.

Abhainn Àirigh nan Sìdhean   G.—River of the sheiling of the little knolls (?) fairies
Abhainn a' Mhuilinn   G.—Mill river
Abhainn Araig   G.—River   N.—River port
Abhainn Bhogaidh   G.—River of the muddy/boggy place
Abainn Ghil   G.—River of   N.—Gully
Abhainn Ghlas   G.—Grey/green river
Abhainn Lussa   A.—Fertility goddess river cf. lus -a plant
Abhainn Phroaig   G.—River of   N.—Broad bay
Abhainn Staoin   G.—River of   N.—Stone
Àirde Chaol   G.—Narrow height/promontory
Àirde Reamhar   G.—Lush growth/great height/promontory
Àirde Thorrinnis   G.—Height of Thori's ness/promontory
(An) Aird Mheadhonach   G.—Mid height/promontory
Àirigh an t-Sluic   G.—Sheiling of the pit/marshy spot
Àirigh Dhubh   G.—Black/dark sheiling
Àirigh Ghlas   G.—Grey/green sheiling
Àirigh Ghutharaidh   G./N.—Godfrey's sheiling
Àirigh Liath   G.—Grey/hoary sheiling
Àirigh nam Biast   G.—Animal sheiling
Àirigh nan clach (or cloch)   G.—Stoney sheiling
Àirigh nan Sidhean   G.—Sheiling of the little knolls
Allallaidh   A.—meaning uncertain: probably contains àl = cliff   G.—Great cliff place
Allt a' Chromain   G.—Stream with the bend or Kite stream
Allt an Daimh   G.—Stream of the stag
Allt an Fhaing Ghairbh   G.—Stream of the   N.—Rough meadow (probably not G.—fang—sheep fank)
Allt Craobhach   G.—Tree-lined stream
Allt Gleann Loch nam Breac   G.—Stream of the glen of the trout loch
Allt Mór   G.—Big stream
Allt na Coite   G.—Little boat stream
Allt na Criche   G.—Boundary stream
Allt na Gamhna   G.—Stream of the stirk
Allt na Muice   G.—Stream of the pig
Allt nan Àirighean   G.—Stream of the sheilings
Allt na tri-dail (pron. driodal) meaning doubtful (i) G.—Stream of the three-fold division (ii) G.—Stream of the   N.—Tree dale (All explanations are unsatisfactory)
Allt Tràigh Leacail   G.—Stream of hill-slope strand
Àlsaig   N.—Sloping harbour
Amand and Àmanta   N.—Confluence

Aoradh (?) G.—Bruthach an Aoraidh—Place of (sun) worship (the accepted derivation) or (ii) N./G/—(?) Gravel place

Ardbeg (An Àird Bheag) G.—Little height/promontory

Ardilistry G.—Height . . . doubtful

Ardimmersay G.—Height . . . doubtful

Ardlarach (Àrd Làrach) G.—High site (probably)

Ardmore (An Àird Mhór) G.—Great height/promontory

Ardnahoe (Àird na h-Uamha G.—Height/promontory of the cave

Ardnave (pron. as in "knave") G.—Height of the A.—(heathen) temple or of St Nemh.

Àrd Talla G.—Rock height

Àros N.—River mouth (G.—dwelling has been suggested but is less likely)

Aruadh (An Atha Ruadh) G.—Red ford

Auchnaclach (Achadh nan Clach) G.—Stone field

Avenvogie (Abhainn Bhogaidh) River of the muddy/boggy place

Avinlussa (Abhainn Lussa) which

Bachlaig G.—Curve place—bachull is a crozier

(Na) Badagan G.—The tufts i.e. place difficult to walk on because of the little hillocks

Bàgh an Dà Dhorus G.—Bay of the two entries

Baile Neachtain G.—Nechtan's township

Balaclava a modern name

Balemeanach (Baile Meadhonach) G.—Mid town

Ballechlavan (Baile a' Chlamhain) G.—Buzzard township or N.—Rift G.—township

Ballemartin (Baile Mhàrtuinn) G.—Martin's township

Ballemony (Baile a' Mhonaidh) G.—Township of the moor

Balletarsin (Baile Tarsuinn) G.—Township on the (hill) slope

Ballevicar (Baile a' Bhiocaire) G.—The Vicar's township

Ballygrant (Baile Gràna) G.—Grain township, Store township

Balole (Bail' Ol) G./N.—Olaf's township

Baluilve (Bail' Uilbh) G./N/—Ulfr's township

Banaltrum Mhór G.—lit. Great nurse, i.e. good rearing ground

Barr G.—Summit but see Chapter VII

Batachan Bàna probably N.—damp places and G.—fair

Bealach Corrach G.—The steep hill-pass

Bealach Gaoth an Ear G.—Pass of the east wind

Beinn a' Chùirn G.—Mountain of the cairn

Beinn Bhiocaire G.—Vicar's mountain (see Note 1 p. 112)

Beinn Bhiorach G.—Pointed mountain

Beinn Bhreac G.—Speckled mountain

Beinn Chùrlaich G.—Gravelly mountain

Beinn Ghibach G.—Rough, tufty mountain

Beinn Leathaig (?) Leathaid G.—Slope mountain

Beinn na Heraibh G.—Mountain of the N.—heights

Beinn nam Fitheach G.—Mountain of the Ravens

Beinn Roineach (recte -ich) G.—Bracken mountain

Beinn Sholum G.—Mountain of the N.—Sheep hill

Beinn Tart a' Mhill G.—Mountain of N.—Hart fell

Beinn Thrasda G.—Diagonal mountain

Beinn Uraraidh G.—Mountain A.—(?) Boundary place, i.e. between Cinel Aenghuis and the other folks

Biod nan Sgarbh G.—Cormorant point

Blàr Buidhe G.—Yellow field

Boghachan Móra G.—Greet reefs (borrowing from Norse)

Boglach nan Tarbh G.—Bull bog

Bolsay N.—Farm

Borrachill A.—Very high place (see p. 37)

Bowmore (Bogha Mór) G.—Great reef (borrowing from Norse)

Brahunisary N. or N./G.—meaning doubtful (?) Brae of Huni's sheiling.
Bridgend (G.—Beul an Atha) Mouth of the Ford
Bruichladdich (Bruthach a' Chladaich) G.—Brae of the shore
Bruthach Mór G.—Big Brae
Bun Abhainne G.—River mouth (Port Wemyss)
Bun an Uillt G.—Mouth of the Stream (Lit. bottom . . .)
Bunnahabhain (Bun na h-Abhainne) G.—River mouth (Lit. bottom . . .) (an old gen.)
Cachaileith Mhór G.—Big gate
Callumkill (Cill' Chaluim-Chille) G.—St. Columba's church
Cam Sgeir (?) N.—Ridge skerry or G.—Crooked skerry
Caolas nan Gall G.—Lowlanders'/foreigners' channel
Caolas Port na Lice G.—Channel of the bay of the flat stone
Caol Ila (recte Ile) G.—Sound of Islay (name given during 19th century to distillery at
    Ruadh-phort G.—Red bay)
(An) Càrn G.—The Cairn
(An) Càrnan G.—Little cairn
Càrn Beannachd G.—Cairn of Blessing, probably by folk etomology for older beannach—
    peaked, horned
Càrn Chonas-àirigh G.—Hill of the gorse sheiling
Carnduncan (Càrn Donnchaidh) G.—Duncan's cairn
Càrn Mór Ghrasdail G—Big cairn (of) N.—Grass dale
Càrn nan Gillean G.—Cairn of the lads probably by folk etymology for Cairn of the N.—
    Gullies
Carrabus N.—Copse or brushwood farm
Carraig an ratha G.—Lucky sea-rock, i.e. good for fishing (probably though rath can be a
    fort too)
Carraig Bhàn G.—Fair sea-rock
Carraig Dhubh G.—Black sea-rock
Carraig Fhada G.—Long sea-rock
Carraig Mhór G.—Great sea-rock
Carraig nam Fear G.—Sea-rock of the men
Cattadale N.—Wild-cat dale (p. 82)
Ceann Caol (Texa) The fine end, being the opposite of
Ceann Garbh (Texa) G.—The rough end
Cille Rònain G.—St. Ronan's church
Clach-àirigh (better Cloch-àirigh) G.—Stone sheiling—an old name
Clach an Tiompain G.—Stone of the Cymbal
Clach Mhic ghillean G.—MacLean's stone
Cladach Fionn G.—Fair shore
Claggan (Claigeann) G.—Fertile field
Cnoc a' Chaoruinn G.—Rowan-tree hill
Cnoc a' Cheàird G.—Tinker's/tradesman's hill
Cnoc a' Chlaidheimh G.—Hill of the sword
Cnoc a' Chorr-bhealaich G.—Hill of the rough pass
Cnoc a' Chùil probably G.—Hill and N.—knob
Cnoc a' Chùirn G.—Hill of the cairn
Cnoc a' Ghamhna Chaim G.—Hill of the one-eyed stirk
Cnoc an Fhamhair G.—Giant's Hill see Drolsay
Cnoc an Fhraoich-Shugain G.—Heather rope hill
Cnoc an Tighe G.—House hill
Cnoc an t-Samhlaidh G.—(?) Ghost hill (?) oddly shaped hill
Cnoc an t-Sleibh G.—Upland plain hill
Cnoc Bhi-bhuirn doubtful see text (p. 77)
Cnoc Chroisprig G.—Hill N.—Cross slope
Cnoc Bhrannabuis G./N.—Hill of Brian's farm
Cnoc Breac G.—Speckled hill
Cnoc Dhiarmaid G.—Diarmid's hill

Cnoc Donn   G.—Brown hill
Cnoc Dronnach   G.—Ridged hill
Cnoc Dubh   G.—Black hill
Cnoc Garbh a' Mhill   doubtful (?)   G.—Rough hill of the   N.—Fell or   G./N.—Chasm hill
Cnoc Grianail   G.—Sunny hill
Cnoc Liath   G.—Grey hill
Cnoc Mór na Claiginn (recte. a' Chlaiginn)   G.—Big hill of the good field
Cnoc na Buaile   G.—Hill of the cattle-fold
Cnoc na Cloiche-muilinn   G.—Millstone hill
Cnoc na Craoibhe   G.—Tree hill
Cnoc na Croise   G.—Cross hill
Cnoc na h-Éilde   G.—Hill of the hind
Cnoc na Faire   G.—Look-out hill
Cnoc na h-Uamha   G.—Cave hill
Cnoc na Nathrach   G.—Serpent hill
Cnoc nan Geòidh   G.—Hill of the geese (for C. nan Geadh)
Cnoc na Piobaireachd   G.—Hill of the bag-pipe playing
Cnoc na Seilge   G.—Hill of the hunt
Cnoc Raonasdail   G.—Hill   N.—Rowan dale
Cnoc Reamhar   G.—Big hill or lush hill
Cnoc Uamh nam Fear   G.—Hill of the Men's cave
Cnoc Undail   G.—Hill   N.—Dog dale
Coille   G.—Forest
Coille a' Ghuail   G.—Charcoal forest
Coille Mhór   G.—the Big Forest
Coille na Dàlach   Dail forest G.—see Dail
Coille nam Bruthach   G.—Forest of the braes
(An) Coire   G.—lit. Cauldron, i.e. pot-shaped depression, corry
Coire a' Chinn-chlach   G.—Corry of the Head-stone
Coire Odhar   G.—the dun corry
Coire Sgiathach   G.—the sheltered corry
Conas-airigh   G.—Gorse sheiling
Conisby   N.—King's estate
Cornabus   N.—Corn farm
Corra-Ghoirtean   G.—the steep little garden, or the Heron garden
Corran Bàn   G.—the Fair curve. lit. sickle
Corrary (Corr àirigh)   G.—The sheiling on the slope
Coulabus   N.—Round hill farm
Cragabus   N.—(see Chap. VII)
Creagach   G.—Craggy place
Creag a' Chait   G.—Rock of the cat
Creagan Loisgte   G.—Parched/burnt rocks
Craigens   G.—with Eng. plural, the rocks, crags
Creag Fhada   G.—Long rock
Creag Fhinn   G.—Fionn's rock
Creag Loisgte   G.—Burnt/parched rock
Creag Mhór   G.—Great rock
Creag Mhór na Faing   G.—Big rock of the sheep fank
Crò Earraich   G.—Spring-time cattle-fold
Crois Mhór   G.—Great cross (Where's the cross?)
(An) Crois sgeir   G./N.—Cross reef
Cruach   G.—Rough hill
Cruach Mhór   G.—Big rough hill
Cruaidh Ghleann   G.—probably "difficult to work" glen lit. hard glen
Cultorsay   N.—Round hill of Thori's farm
Cultun   (see Chapter VII)   meaning doubtful

116

Cùrlach   G.—Gravel place
(An) Curran   G.—(?) Piece of land
Daill (an Dàil)   G.—Focal-point place, chief centre see p. 103
Diollaid nam Fiadh   G.—Saddle of the deer
Doire Fhearna   G.—Alder grove
Doire Liath   G.—Grey grove
(An) Doirlinn   G.—Isthmus flooded at high tide
Doodilmore   G.—Big   N.—Bog dale
Drochaid Bheag   G.—Little Bridge
Drochaid Tioram   G.—Dry Bridge
Drolsay   N.—Troll's river cf. Cnoc an Fhamhair
Duisker   N.—Cairn rock
Druim Àladh   G.—Speckled ridge
Druim an Stuin   G.—Ridge of the   N.—Stone
Druim an Uisge Fhuair   G.—Cold-water ridge
Druim Buidhe   G.—Yellow ridge
Druim Claigeann Mhicheil   G.—Ridge of Michael's good field
Druim Dubh   G.—Black ridge
Druim Fada   G.—Long ridge
Druim Iriseig   G.—(?) The ridge with the little irregularity
Druim Meadhonach   G.—Middle ridge
Druim Mór   G.—Great ridge
Druim na Croise   G.—Cross ridge
Druim na h-Earasaid   G.—Ridge of the (woman's) plaid (probably by folk etymology) for
      N.—Ari's farm
Druim nan Cnàmh   G.—Ridge of the bones
Druim nan Crann   G.—Ridge of the trees (?masts, ?ploughs)
Druim nan Each   G.—Horse ridge
Druim Scaraba   probably G./N.—Barren ridge
Druim Seasg   G.—Infertile ridge
Druim Teamhair   G.—Pleasant ridge
Dubh Loch   G.—Dark/black loch
(An) Dùn   G.—the fort
Dùn a' Mhullaich Bhàin   G.—Fort of the fair summit
Dùn Bhorreraig   G.—Fort of   N.—Fort Harbour
Dùn Bhruichlinn   G.—Bricriu's fort (probably) see page 38
Dùn Chollapus   doubtful (?) G.—Fort of   N.—Koll's farm
Dùn Fhinn   G.—Fionn's fort
Dùn Glas an Lòin Ghuirm   G.—Grey fort of the green meadow
Dùn Guaidhre   N.—Godred's   G.—fort
Dùn Lossit   A.—(see Chapter IV)
Dùn Mideir   G.—Midir's fort
Dùn Mór Ghil   G.—Big fort of the   N.—Gully
Dùn nan Nighean   G.—Fort of the maidens
Dùn Nòsbrig   G.—Fort   N.—Fort on the crag
Dùich   G.—Black meadow
Eilean a' Chùirn   G.—Cairn island
Eilean an t-Sluic   G.—Isle of the marsh or trench
Eilean an Tannais Sgeir   G.—Island of the   N.—high ness reef
Eilean Beag   G.—Little island
Eilean Cam   G.—Crooked island
Eilean Craobhach   G.—Wooded island
(An t-) Eilean Cruinn   G.—The round island
Eilean Liath   G.—Grey island
Eilean Mhic Coinnich   G.—Mackenzie's island (probably a corruption of an older name)
Eilean Mhic Mhaolmhuire   G.—Island of the son of Maolmuire (servant of Mary)
Eilean na Muice Duibhe   G.—Island of the black pig

Eilean nan Caorach G.—Sheep island
Eilean nan Gobhar G.—Goat island
Eilean nan Uan G.—Lamb island
Eilean na Sgioba G.—Island of the N.—Ship river
Eilean Nòstaig G.—Island of the N.—East bay
Elister (?) N.—(see Chapter VII)
Emeraconart (Iomaire Chòmhnard) G.—the level rig
Eorrabus N.—Gravel bank farm
Eresaid (?) N.—Ari's steading
Esknish A.—Water meadow
Fangdu (Fang Dubh) G.—Black N.—meadow
Fang Poll a' Chapuill N./G.—Field of the mare's bog
Farkin (Paircean) G.—Little park
(Am) Fàsach G.—The moor
(An) Fhaing Gharbh G.—The rough sheep fank
Fionn Phort G.—Fair haven
Feur Lochan G.—Little grassy loch
Gartaharra (Gart a' Charraigh) G.—Standing-stone garden
Gartbreac (Gart Breac) G.—Speckled garden
Gartloist (Gart Loisgte) G.—Burnt, parched garden
Gartmain (Gart Meadhoin) G.—Mid garden (cf. N.—Miðgarðr)
Gartnatra (Gart na Tràghad) G.—Garden by the beach
Gearach probably G.—Short field but a Norse origin has been suggested
Geodha Ghille Mhoire G.—Gilmour's creek
Geodha nam Mult G.—Wethers' creek
Geodha nan Cuilean G.—Creek of the whelps
Giùr Bheinn N.—Cleft G.—Mountain
Glacan Daraich G.—Little dell of the oak
Glac na Criche G.—Narrow valley of the boundary
Glais Uig N.—Sea harbour
Gleann a' Chapuill Bhàin G.—Glen of the white mare
Gleann a' Chàrdaidh G.—Glen of the (?) carding
Gleann a' Cheardaich (recte. na Ceardaich) G.—Glen of the smithy
Gleann Àirigh an t-Sluic G.—Glen of the sheiling of the pit or marsh
Gleann Àsdail (Astle) G.—Glen N.—Ridge dale
Gleann an Dòbhrain G.—Otter glen
Gleann Bun an Easa G.—The glen at the foot of the waterfall
Gleann Choireadail G.—Glen G./N.—Cauldron dale
Gleann Droighneach G.—Thorn glen
Gleann Dubh G.—Dark/black glen
Gleann Ghàireasdail G.—Glen of N.—Gerdi's dale
Gleann Leòra G.—Glen of the N.—Muddy river
Gleann Loch nam Breac G.—Glen of the trout loch
Gleann na Caillich G.—Glen of the old woman (the goddess)
Gleann nam Meirleach G.—Thieves' glen (But why?)
Gleann Maraiche G.—Scurvy-grass glen
Gleann Mhàrtuin G.—Martin's glen
Gleann Tuath G.—North glen
Glenegedale (Gleann Eigeadail) G.—Glen N.—Oak dale
Glen Golach (Gleann Gobhlach) G.—Forked glen
Glen Machrie (Gleann a' Mhachaire—for na machrach) G.—Glen of the coastal plain
Glennagaoith apparently for G.—MacKay's glen
Gortanilivorrie (Gortan Tigh Ghille-Mhuire) G.—Garden of Gilmour's house
Gortantaoid (Gortan Taoid) G.—Garden of the cord, but why? cf. Tigh nan Teud (Perthshire
Grainel N.—Green field
Grianan G.—Sunny place

118

Gròbolls   N.—Groa's farm
Gruineart   N.—Shallow loch
Grùlin   doubtful but the name occurs also in Mull and Skye
Guala Dhubh   G.—Black shoulder (corner of mountain)
Gualann an Sgairibh   G.—Shoulder of the G./N.—rock
(na) Hearadh   N.—the Heights
Imeraval (Iomair a' Mhail)   G.—Rental rig
Ilistry   doubtful
Immersay   doubtful
Iomallach   G.—Outermost (rock)
Iseanach Mor   G.—The big chicks, i.e. the rocks
Islay (Ile)   A.—(see p. 28)
Keills (Cill Chaluim-Chille)   St. Columba's church
Kelsay (Ceallsa)   N.—Keel farm, i.e. standing-stone farm cf. Callernish (Lewis) Standing-
    stone ness
Kentraw (Cionn Tràghad)   G.—End of the strand
Keppols (Ceapasadh)   N.—(?) Place, farm of the gatherings of people
Kilarrow (Cill a Rubha)   G.—Maol Rubha's church
Kilbride (Cille Bride)   G.—St. Bride's church
Kilchiaran (Cille Chiarain)   G.—St. Ciaran's church
Kilchoman (Cille Chomain)   G.—St. Coman's church
Kilellan (Cill Fhaolain)   G.—St. Faolan's church
Kilennan (Cill Fhionain)   G.—St. Finnen's church
Killenallan (Cille an Àilein)   G.—Church on the green sward
Kilmeny (Cille Mheanaidh)   G.—Church of ?. Possibly Eithne mother of Columba but a
    saint otherwise unknown is more probable
Kilnaughton (Cill Neachtain)   (N. is usually elided locally) Naitan's church
Kilslevan (Cill Sleimhin)   Slevan's church (a follower of Columba)
Kindrochaid (Cionn Drochaid)   G.—Bridge end (not the village—Beul an Atha)
Knockangle Point (Cnoc Aingeil)   G.—Fire hill
Knocklearach (Cnoc Chléireach)   G.—Clerics' hill
Kynagarry   N.—meaning uncertain (?) Hillside (cheek) farm
Lagavullin (Lag a' Mhuilinn)   G.—Mill hollow
Lag Dearg   G.—Red hollow
Lag na Criche   G.—Boundary hollow
Lag nan Capull   G.—Mares' hollow
Lag Odhar   G.—Grey hollow
Lamh-bheinn   Doubtful. Possibly N.—hlað stack and   G.—mountain
Langadail   N.—Long dale
Laorin (Laorean)   N.—Mud flat
Laphroaig   doubtful. Probably N.
Leacann a' Chnuic   G.—Steep slope of the hill
Leac Bhuidhe   G.—Flat yellow rock
Leac Eithne   G.—Flat ivy-covered rock (probably)
Leac nan Laogh   G.—Flat rock of the calves
Leana na Feannaige   G.—Meadow of the rig (?) crow
Leck Gruineart (Leac Gruineirt)   G.—Flat rock of   N.—the shallow loch.
Lenovore (Leana Mhór)   G.—Big meadow (gender unusual)
Loch a' Bhealaich Àird   G.—Loch of the high hill-pass
Loch a' Chaoruinn   G.—Rowan loch
Loch a' Chaidheimh   G.—Loch of the sword
Loch a' Chnuic   G.—Loch of the hill
Loch a' Chnuic Bhric   G.—Loch of the speckled hill
Loch Àirigh Dhaibhidh   G.—Loch of David's sheiling
Loch Àirigh nan Caisteal   G.—Loch of the sheiling of the castles (But why is it plural?)
Loch a' Mhala   G.—Loch of the brow of the hill
Loch a' Mhuilinn-Ghaoithe   G.—Windmill loch

Lochan Broach   G.—Foul loch
Loch na Dubhaich   G.—meaning doubtful (?) Dark meadow loch
Loch an Fhir Mhóir   G.—Loch of the big man (But who was he?)
Loch an Raoin   G.—Loch of the moor
Loch an t-Sàilein   G.—Arm of the sea
Loch Arish   G.—meaning doubtful (?) loch of the exposed (difficult) ford
Loch Bharradail   G.—Loch of the   N.—Border dale
Loch Bhogaidh   G.—Loch of the soft ground
Loch Cam   G.—Crooked loch
Loch Càrn a' Mhaoil   G.—Loch of the bare hill cairn
Loch Càrn nan Gall   Loch of the foreigners' cairn
Loch Clach a' Bhuaile   G.—Loch of the cattle-fold stone
Loch Conailbhe   A.—Loch of the goddess
Loch Corr (Cobhair)   G.   Frothy loch (not "crooked")
Loch Dearg an Sgorra   G.—Red loch of the steep hill
Loch Dhòmhnaill   G.—Donald's loch
Loch Dubh   G.—Black loch
Loch Éidhinn   G.—Ivy loch
Loch Finlaggan   G.—St. Finlaggan's loch
Loch Gorm   G.—Blue loch
Loch Iarnan   G.—Probably Loch of the Sloes
Loch Leathann   G.—Broad loch
Loch Leathann an Sgorra   G.—Broad loch of the steep hill
Loch an Leinibh   G.—the Baby's loch
Loch Leódamais   G.—Loch of   N.—Leod's moss
Loch Mhurchaidh   G.—Murchadh's loch
Loch na Beinne   G.—Loch of the mountain
Loch na Beinne Brice   G.—Loch of the speckled mountain
Loch na Làthaich   G.—Bog loch
Loch nan Ban   G.—Women's loch
Loch nam Breac   G.—Trout loch
Loch nam Manaichean (pron. Mainichean) G.—meaning doubtful. Possibly a form of
   Mainnir—pen or fold for animals hence Loch of the cattle-folds
Loch nan Caorach   G.—Sheep loch
Loch nan Diol (Giol)   G.—said to be Leech loch
Loch nan Gillean   G.—The Lads loch or   G.—loch of the   N.—Gullies
Loch nan Gobhar   G.—Goats' loch
Lochan na Nigheadaireachd   G.—Little loch where washing is done
Loch Shibhin   G.—Bullrush loch (?) Venison loch is possible. The true meaning is lost
Loch Sholuim   G.—Loch of the   N.—Sheep hill
Loch Smigeadail   G.—Loch   N.—doubtful see text Ch. 7
Loch Staoisha   G.—Loch   N.—Stone river
Lòn Bàn   G.—Fair Meadow
Lòn Brothach   G.—Foul meadow
Lorgbà   G.—lit. Cattle shank, i.e. a shank-shaped piece of land fit for cattle. cf. Lurgyndaspok
   (Lorg an Easbuig) given in 1391 for a piece of land in N.E. Scotland
Lorg Réidh   G.—Smooth/level piece of land. cf. Lorgba
Lossit (Lossaid)   (see p. 35)
Luig an Tairbh   G.—Bull Dells
Lyrabus (Laorabus)   N.—Muddy farm
(Am) Mala   Brow of the hill
Mala Bholsa   G.—Brow of the hill of the   N.—Farm
Maoile Mhòr   G.—Big hill-face
Maol a' Bharra   G.—Bare hill of the summit,
Maol Àirigh o' Dhuin   G.—Bare hill of O'Dweeny's sheiling
Maol an Fhithich   G.—Bare hill of the raven
Maol an Tairbh   G.—Bare hill of the bull

120

Maol Beag   G.—Little bare hill
Maol Buidhe   G.—Bare yellow hill
Maol Bun an Uillt   G.—Bare hill above the mouth of the stream
Maol Chnoc   G.—Bare hill
Maol Mheadhoin   Middle bare hill
Maol na Coille   G.—Bare hill of the forest
Maol nan Caorach   G.—Bare hill of the sheep
Maol nan Eun   G.—Bare hill of the birds
Maol nan Gobhar   G.—Bare hill of the goats
Margadale   N.—meaning doubtful 1. Market dale (said to have been the slave market); 2. Forest dale; 3. Border/boundary dale
(Am) Meall   G.—Hill, mound
(Am) Miadar   G.—Meadow
Mòine a' Choire   G.—Moor of the dell
Mòine Liath   G.—Grey peat-bog
Mòine Mhór   G.—Big bog
Mòine na Sùrdaig   G.—Moor of the (?) leaping. Many ingenious explanations given. Probably from sord=sward cf. Swords near Dublin. If "leap" then the bog so soft that one leaps from tussock to tussock
Mòine nam Faoileann   G.—Seagull moor
Mòine Riabhach   G.—Brindled moor
Mulindry   Doubtful. Apparently an old Locative containing "mill"
(Am) Mullach Bàn   G.—Fair Summit
Mullach Dubh   G.—Black summit
Mullach Mór   G.—Great summit
Mulris (Maol Ris)   G.—Exposed hill-slope
Muran (Murach) a' Mhachaire (na Machrach)   G.—Sand hills of the machir
Nerabus   N.—Nether farm
Neriby   N.—Knorr's estate
Octofad   G.—Long eighth farm (An t-Ochdamh Fada)
Octomore (An t-Ochdamh Mor)   G.—Big eighth farm
Octovullin (Ochdamh a' Mhuilinn)   G.—Mill eighth farm
Oitir nam Bó   G.—Cattle sandspit
Olistadh   N.—Olaf's farm
Or-said (steading on Orsay)   G./N.—Oran's steading
Pàirc Dhubh   G.—Black park
Pàirc Mhór (Mhic an Aba)   G.—(MacNab's) big park (He is said to have taken the land during the 19th century)
(Na) Peileirean   G.—The bullets (descriptive of the rocks)
Persabus   N.—Priest's farm
Pliadan Dubha   G.—Dark/black plots of ground
(Am) Plodan   G.—Little pool
Plod Sgeirean   G.—Still water reefs
Poll an Dubhaidh   G.—Pool of . . . (?)
Poll Gorm   G.—Blue/green pool
Port an Eas   G.—Waterfall bay/harbour
Port an Ladhair   G.—Hoof harbour/bay
Port an Tobair   G.—Harbour/bay of the well
Port an t-Seilich   G.—Willow-tree bay/harbour
Port an t-Sruthain   G.—Bay/harbour of the stream
Port Asabuis   G.—Bay/harbour of   N.—Ridge farm
Port Askaig   G.—Bay/harbour   N.—Ash-tree harbour
Port Bun Aibhne   G.—River-mouth Bay/harbour
Port Carraig Sgairn   G.—Bay/harbour of the sea-rock where the stones roll noisily
Port Charlotte   modern called after Lady Charlotte Campbell. Anciently Port Sgioba G.— Bay/harbour of   N.—Ship river
Port Dòmhnaill Chruinn   G.—Plump Donald's bay/harbour

121

Port Ellen modern-called after Lady Eleanor Campbell. Anciently Leodamus N.—Leod's moss

Port Fròige G.—Bay/harbour of the recess

Port Mias-sgeir G.—Bay/harbour of the N.—Narrow skerry/reef

Port na Cille G.—Bay of the Church

Port na Diollaide G.—Bay/harbour of the saddle

Portnahaven (Port na h-Abhainne) G.—Bay/harbour of the river

Port na Lice G.—Bay/harbour of the flat stone

Port nan Gallan G.—Bay/harbour of the coltsfoot. (So explained but "gallan" has other meanings)

Port Wemyss modern name. Anciently Bun Abhainne G.—River mouth

Proaig N.—Broad Bay/harbour

Raineach Mhór G.—Great fern place

Réidh a' Bhuirg G.—Level place of the N.—Fort

Risabus N.—Brushwood farm

Robolls (Robollsa) N.—Rough land farm

Rudha a' Bhuic G.—Promontory of the buck

Rudha a' Chladaich G.—Promontory of the shore

Rudha a' Chlàdain G.—Meaning doubtful. Promontory of the (i) oar guard (ii) fence of stone (iii) spume

Rudha a' Chùirn G.—Promontory of the cairn

Rudha a' Ghuail G.—Coal/charcoal promontory

Rudha a' Mhàil G./N.—(?) (see Chapter VII)

Rudha a' Mhullaich Bhàin G.—Promontory of the fair summit

Rudha an Aonain-Luachrach G.—Promontory of the rushy moor

Rudha an Dùin G.—Promontory of the fort

Rudha an t-Sàile G.—Promontory of the sea water

Rudha a' Phuirt Bhàin G.—Promontory of the fair bay/harbour

Rudha a' Phuirt Mhóir G.—Promontory of the big bay/harbour

Rudha Bhachlaig G.—Crozier-shaped promontory (not obviously so)

Rudha Bholsa G.—Promontory of the N.—Farm

Rudha Bhoreraig G.—Promontory of the N.—Fort harbour

Rudha Biorach G.—Pointed promontory

Rudha Dubh Allt na Muice G.—Black promontory of the pig's stream

Rudha Geodha nam Mult G.—Promontory of the wethers' creek

Rudha Glas G.—Grey promontory

Rudha Lamanais G./N.—(see Chapter VII)

Rudha Leac an Fheòir G.—Promontory of the grassy slope/flat stone

Rudha Leac nan Laogh G.—Promontory of the Calves' Slope/flat stone

Rudha Liath G.—Grey promontory

Rudha Luidhnis G.—Promontory of the N.—(?) Low ness

Rudha Mór G.—Great Promontory

Rudha na Gainmhich G.—Promontory of the sand

Rudha na Fainge G.—Promontory of the sheep-fank

Rudha na h-Àirde Móire G.—Promontory of the great height

Rudha Port an t-Seilich G.—Promontory of the Willow-tree bay/harbour

Rudha Ruadh G.—Red Promontory

Rudha Ruighinn G.—Probably=ruighe—Mountain-fort promontary

(An) Ruime G.—from N.—Open stretch of ground

(An) Rumach G.—the bog

Saligo N.—(?) Seal creek

Sannaig Mór/Beag G.—Great/small N.—Sand harbour

Scànlastle Probably a personal name with N.—Dale

Scarrabus N.—Rocky-ridge farm

Sean-chlaigeann G.—long-cultivated meadow (sometimes—formerly cultivated)

Sgaireil N.—Hill at the edge

Sgeir a' Chlachain G.—The village reef

Sgeirean Buidhe Ghil G.—Yellow reefs of N.—the gully
Sgeirean Dubha G.—Black reefs
Sgeirean Leathann G.—Broad reefs
Sgeirean Tràghaidh G.—Reefs of the ebbing tide
Sgeir Fhada G.—Long reef
Sgeir nam Ban G.—The women's reef
Sgeir na Nighinn G.—Daughter's/maiden's reef
Sgeir nan Sgarbh G.—Cormorant reef
Sgeir nan Sligean G.—Reef of the shells
Sgeir Phlocach G.—Humped reef
Sgioba N.—Ship river
Sgorr nam Faoileann G.—Steep hill of the Seagulls.
Shun Bheinn N.—Knob G.—Mountain
Sleivemore (Sliabh Mór) G.—Big hill-slope
Sleivevin G.—meaning doubtful (?) Slippery hill-slope
Sliabh a' Mheallaidh G.—Hill slope of the deception
Sliabh Aom G.—the sloping moor
Sliabh Bhrothain (doubtful)
Sliabh Mór G.—Great hill-slope
Sliabh nam Feur Lochan G.—Hill slope of the grassy lochs
Sliabh nan Coisichean G.—Hill slope of the walkers(But why?)
Slochd Mhaol Doiridh G.—Maol Doiridh's pit
Slugaide Glas G.—Grey quagmire
Smaull N.—Little cliff
Solum N.—Sheep hill
(An) Sopachan G.—(?) Place of the wispy heather
Srath Bhata probably N.—Wet G.—strath, glen
Srath Luachrach G.—Rushy strath/glen
Sròn Dubh G.—Black/dark headland (lit. nose)
Sruthan Rabhairt G.—Chattering streamlet
Sruthan Ruadh G.—Little red stream
Staoisha N.—Stone river
Storakaig N.—meaning uncertain (i) Big strip (ii) Peat strip (with prothetic s-)
Stremnish N.—Current point
Stuadh Runasta G.—Pillar N.—meaning doubtful. Either from hraun — Rough pillar or a
    participle of hrynja — Toppling pillar
Tais bheinn G.—Dank mountain
Tallant (Tàlanta) probably N.—High land but it has been suggested that this is Tailte as in
    Teltown, Ireland.
(An) Tàmhanachd G.—Long slope
Tarr Sgeir N.—High G.—reef
Tayvullin (Tigh a' Mhuilinn) G.—Mill house
Texa N.—meaning doubtful
Tigh an Arbhair G.—Corn house
Tigh na Beinne G.—House of the mountain
Tighnacachla (Tigh na Cachaileith) G.—Gatehouse
Tigh na Speur (modern) Sky house
Tivaagain (Tir Mhathagan) G.—Land of the (?) bears
Tobar Chairistiona Chaimbeul G.—Cairistiona Campbell's well
Tobar Haco N.—Haco's G. Well
Tobar Muireig (Texa) Little St. Mary's well
Tom nan Crior (criathair) Pot-hole hill
Ton Àirigh Sgallaidh G.—Blunt headland of the sheiling of Sgallaidh (meaning doubtful)
Ton Lagain G.—Blunt promontory of the little hollow
Ton Mór G.—Big blunt headland
Tormisdale N.—Norman's dale
Torra doubtful G.—Hillocks, but here, more probably N.—Horn river

123

Torr a' Chreamha G.—Wild garlic hill
Torrain Dubha G.—Little black/dark knolls
Torran G.—Hillocks
Toranore (Torran Odhar) G.—Grey hillock
Torr Dubh G.—Black hill
Torr na Carraige G.—Hillock of the sea-rock
Tràigh an Luig G.—Strand of the hollow
Tràigh a' Mhachaire (for T. na Machrach) Machir strand
Tràigh Bhaile Aonghuis G.—the Strand of Angus' township
Tràigh Bhàn G.—Fair strand—referring to colour
Tràigh Cill a Rubha G.—Strand of St. Maolrubha's church
Tràigh Fleisgein Strand of fleisgean. This word is said to mean "noise".
Tràigh Leacail G.—Hill-slope strand
Tràigh nan Cisteachan G.—Strand of the boxes
Tràigh Nòstaig G.—Strand of the N. East Bay
Trùdernish N.—doubtful meaning (see Chapter 4)
Uamhannan Donna G.—Brown caves
Uamh nam Fear G.—The men's cave
Uisge an t-Suidhe G.—Water of the resting-place. Funerals used to halt here
Uisge Gleann a' Chromain G.—Water of the Glen of the hump
Uisge na Criche G.—Water of the boundary
Uillt Ruadha G.—Red streams